Praying for Restraint:

Frequent Flying with an Inner-City Hospital CNA

Hi Paulette - Congrats on being a giveaway winner! I hope you greatly enjoy this book. Best, Allen Long

a memoir

Allen Long

Legacy Book Press LLC
Camanche, Iowa

Copyright © 2021 Allen Long

Cover photo by Anki Hoglund
Cover design by Kaitlea Toohey (kaitleatoohey.com)

All names and identifying characteristics for most entities and
individuals have been changed. As it is with all personal
narratives, mine is subjective. These stories are told from my
perspective and my memories; I recognize that everyone
remembers events differently.

All rights reserved. No part of this book may be used or
reproduced by any means, graphic, electronic, or mechanical,
including photocopying, recording, taping or by any information
storage retrieval system without the written permission of the
publisher except in the case of brief quotations embodied in
critical articles and reviews.

ISBN: 978-1-7347986-6-1
Library of Congress Case Number: 1-10362420881

SPECIAL THANKS

The author wishes to thank the following people who so generously provided feedback regarding this book: David Bettencourt, Dr. Minda Dudley, Mark Finnigan, Dr. Elisabeth Gallagher, David "Danny" Long, Elizabeth Long, Kit McIlroy, Dr. Arkady Oreper, Dr. Pamela Paradowski, John Rieth, Ben Sawyer-Long, Matt Sawyer-Long, and Dr. Steven Rosenthal.

DEDICATION

To my wife, Elizabeth

And to our children: Matt, Stephanie, Josh, and Ben

CONTENTS

Flight One: 2013 & 2014

Praying for Restraint

First Day

Five years ago, I accepted a position as an assistant nurse at Malmed Memorial, an inner-city "safety net" hospital on the Pacific Coast that admits all patients, regardless of their ability to pay. The facility had the busiest emergency room in the country, it was famous for its outstanding trauma unit, and it was a teaching hospital. I was encouraged by the committed-looking doctors and nurses bustling down the corridors and in and out of patient rooms when I reported for duty.

I stood at the nurses' station trailing my various professions: assistant nurse in elder care, swim team coach, swimming instructor, winery tasting room host, and, far in the past, president of a Silicon Valley high-tech marketing firm. At fifty-seven, I was looking at maybe my last shot at a meaningful career, and I was sick of barely scraping by financially. I couldn't remember the last time I picked up prescriptions, got a haircut, filled up my silver Honda Civic with gas, or took my wife, Elizabeth, to dinner or the movies without first agonizing over whether we could afford the expenditure.

She had, however, insisted on taking me out to our favorite Italian restaurant to celebrate my new job. She'd raised her glass of Rombauer chardonnay in a toast and said, "Here's to my hospital nurse. You'll do great!"

I clinked my glass against hers, full of love. Not only was I buoyed by her good spirits and confidence in me, but I admired the way she so deeply enjoyed celebrating the bright moments in our lives.

Emergency

Two weeks into the job, working the floor in our medical-surgical unit, I responded to a call light. An elderly patient's bony hands gesticulated wildly, but he was unable to speak. Upon closer inspection, I realized he was silent because he was breathing through a surgically created hole and tube in his trachea, a tracheostomy. Scenting copper, I noticed his hospital gown was soaked crimson, blood spurting out of the tracheostomy every one or two seconds. He gasped, struggling to breathe.

I ran to alert his nurse, Joseph Eze, known behind his back as Easy Joe and Slow Mo Joe. I found him in the room where nurses drew patient medications—they were not to be disturbed unless there's an emergency.

He set down the medication he was holding and looked at me through his thick glasses. He slapped his hands to his shaved head and said, "Oh, no! An emergency! What am I going to do? How will I handle it? Can I stand the pressure?"

Then he issued a loud, barking laugh.

Joe pushed past me at his normal leisurely pace, sauntering down the hall to his patient. One of the nurses, Angela Cooper, and I followed him.

He stood impassively watching the patient, who was thrashing and flailing his hands while making desperate choking sounds, blood still arcing from his tracheostomy.

Angela grabbed Slow Mo by his shoulder, imploring him to report the emergency.

Without haste, Joe pulled out his cell phone and dialed.

Finally assured the patient would receive emergency assistance, I continued working the floor, but I circled back to Room 2 a few minutes later just to double-check. Two doctors worked urgently above the patient. Using a vacuum pump, they'd already suctioned nearly a liter of blood from his lungs. Without intervention, he would have drowned in it.

Did we report Joseph Eze? As much as we wanted to, we didn't because Joe was part of a tight-knit clique that extended upward into nursing management.

Blood-Soaked Bed

I had one more run-in with Easy Joe before we ended up working on different floors. As the floor certified nursing assistant (CNA) assigned to all patients on the unit, I spent a hectic day responding to patient call lights and requests for assistance from RNs. Early in my shift, charge nurse, Carmen Sanchez, told me Mrs. Hampton in Room 11 needed to be cleaned up. This usually meant the patient had urinated or had a bowel movement in bed. Or the patient might've just needed a bed bath.

I entered Mrs. Hampton's room, but before I could assess what she needed, Easy Joe kicked me out.

"We've got her," he said, indicating that he and an RN in training, Cecelia Farber, would team up to care for Mrs. Hampton.

I spent the rest of my shift crazy-busy. As we all prepared to punch out at 3:30 p.m., Easy Joe and Cecelia attempted to hand off Mrs. Hampton to an evening-shift RN named Jessica.

Suddenly, Jessica burst from Room 11, cornered me, and said, "Don't you dare punch out, you little weasel, until you've taken proper care of Mrs. Hampton!"

"I don't know what you're talking about," I told her. "Joe and Cecelia have been caring for her all day." I bristled at being scolded, as if by a tyrannical, irresponsible parent.

"That's not what they told me," she said. "They said they asked you to clean her up this morning, and you never touched her."

"That's not true!" I protested. Her shouting unnerved me, as shouting always did. *Was I about to be fired already?*

Hearing the commotion, Carmen approached us to see what our disagreement was about.

We each told her our side of the story. She then grilled Easy Joe and Joyce before leading us to examine Mrs. Hampton, who, it turns out, had lain with a leaking wound in a blood-soaked bed for the entire shift.

Back in the hallway, Carmen pointed at Joe and Joyce. "Shame on you for letting this poor woman lie in a bloody bed all day! And then to blame it on Allen!"

Even though Carmen vindicated me, I trembled with anxiety.

For years, I'd been in psychotherapy with Ginger Lightfoot, who was helping me overcome the PTSD I acquired as the result of childhood physical abuse.

On my worst day as a kid, my father smacked my bare bottom hard twenty-four times with a thick, oak paddle he'd made—the first time he hit me with a store-bought paddle, his blow was so forceful that it snapped it in half. Ginger said that when my parents mistreated me, it was like they were silently screaming at me. Therefore, when colleagues at Malmed Memorial shouted at me, it exacerbated my PTSD, producing panic attacks and the jitters.

Nomads

Before I landed the CNA position at Malmed Memorial, my wife, Elizabeth, and I lived like nomads. During my peak earning years, we'd raised our four kids and two dogs (golden retrievers) in a modest, peach-colored house I loved with a two-thirds of an acre backyard. Elizabeth and I were married on the back deck, and we hosted numerous joyful parties there. When the dotcom bubble burst, forcing me to shutter my business and live on home equity while I unsuccessfully job hunted, Elizabeth and I realized we needed to sell the house.

Unfortunately, the only buyer we were able to attract in the fragile economy was a South American dentist, who freaked out when he learned some of the rooms in the house had been constructed without permits by a previous owner — we were completely up-front about this.

"I'd go to jail!" he said.

He finally agreed to purchase our home on the condition that Elizabeth and I pay all his closing costs as well as our own, so we lost our home as well as $10,000 of profit from its sale.

Next, we rented the home of a friend of a friend, but only for 18 months, until we discovered that we overpaid.

Two major events occurred while we occupied that abode. First, our daughter, Stephanie, was married on the back deck. Second, I had a major panic attack. When I was under treatment in our local hospital's psychiatric ward, my social worker summarized why I was there:

"So let me recap," she said. "You were physically abused as a child, you've held several high-stress business jobs, and you've been fired or laid off from several of them due to unfavorable economics or politics. In addition, you had a fifteen-year unhappy marriage that ended in a bitter divorce. Your youngest son recently underwent brain surgery. You've happily remarried, but your stepdaughter who lives with you deeply resents you for competing for her mother's attention, and her hostility has lasted over a decade. You've lost your business, your home, and you've been unemployed for the last two years. And, until this hospital stay, you had undiagnosed PTSD and anxious depression."

"That about sums it up," I said, perversely impressed by the extensive string of disasters that comprised my life.

After I recovered, we found a two-bedroom condo with the opposite problem as before: now our rent was undervalued, meaning it could be priced out of our means at any time.

So I took the job at Malmed Memorial to achieve long-sought financial stability. At the same time, I wanted to work in a helping profession. I'd had deeply satisfying experiences in this area as a swim team coach, swimming instructor, and college teacher. While I was a grad student at the University of Arizona in Tucson working on my MFA in fiction writing, I taught freshman composition and creative writing, including classes for low-income students who'd attended impoverished high schools.

If these students passed my summer classes with a C or better, they were admitted to the university in the fall; otherwise, they were turned away. Fifty-nine out of my sixty students entered the university and continued as A and B students in English. This is one of my proudest moments, and I decided back then to become a college instructor.

However, I made a fatal mistake; I neglected to add a Ph.D. in English to my credentials, thus unwittingly locking myself out of the college teaching market. Instead, I moved with my first wife, Linda, and our son, Mathew, to the costly San Francisco Bay Area, where Linda had a large extended family. I veered into marketing and competitive strategy for money and dropped out for the same reason.

Baseline

When a new patient arrived on our unit, we'd immediately take her vital signs, even if they'd been taken minutes before on another floor, giving us a baseline on how the patient was doing in our environment.

In this spirit, since my story of Malmed Memorial has also become the story of my marriage, let me offer a baseline reading of Allen and Elizabeth at the time I was hired. Basically, we were happily married, each a safe harbor for the other. After I was abused as a child, I perpetuated the victimization with my first marriage. Elizabeth followed a childhood of face slaps and berating by her mother with marriage to a shy, handsome guy from church who beat and raped her.

In 2017, I took Elizabeth to see the coming-of-age film, *Lady Bird*, starring Saoirse Ronan as Christine "Lady Bird" McPherson and Laurie Metcalf as Marion, Christine's ever-critical mother. I enjoyed the film. When the lights came up, I expected Elizabeth to smile as she does after a good movie, but she was stricken.

"Oh my God," she said. "That was just like seeing the ghost of my mother."

So we'd both been beaten up by life, and we comforted and supported each other. In addition, because of my undiagnosed PTSD and anxious depression, I was filled with a manic need for exercise when we first met, so Elizabeth and I hiked and biked all over the San Francisco Bay Area.

We were happy and fit. At Coyote Hills Regional Park, we often pedaled on an asphalt trail that passed through marshlands and then rose, looping above the San Francisco Bay shoreline. Sunlight glinted off azure water, and we frequently spotted pelicans, egrets, and marsh hawks. After the track veered inland and climbed sharply, we'd pause at the pinnacle to enjoy the spectacular view and golden hills. Then we'd plunge our ten-speeds down the steep incline, laughing in the wind.

The Dog Whisperer

An important aspect of knowing Elizabeth is understanding her relationships with man's best friend. When Elizabeth first stepped into my house in Castro Valley two days after we met and fell in love, she was greeted by my beloved three-year-old golden retriever, Lucy. The two of us, man and beast, were quite close, but Elizabeth

9

patted Lucy's fair head and whispered something that spoke to her very soul, and they instantly bonded, while I was relegated to the proverbial status of chopped liver.

And Elizabeth has usurped the affections of every canine we've owned since and most of the pooches she pet-sits or cares for at the award-winning veterinary clinic where she serves as the head receptionist. All over town, clients stop her to report their mutts' maladies and seek advice. She's approached so often that I joke she's running for mayor.

Finally, Elizabeth can explain complex concepts to dogs, such as Daylight-Saving Time. Let's listen in on a dinnertime conversation she had last autumn with our golden retriever, Ruby.

Ruby: *Orange-brown puppy dog eyes insisting on dinner at 3:00 p.m.*

Elizabeth: "Ruby, I know you think it's four o'clock and time to eat, but it's only three o'clock because we fell back an hour for Daylight Saving Time. Remember this happens every year?"

Ruby: *Cocking her head to the right.*

Elizabeth: "But you're a smart girl—you know it's really four o'clock, don't you?"

Ruby: *Tilting her head to the left.*

Elizabeth: "So here's what we're going to do. I'm going to feed you now, but I'm also going to serve you a little later each day until your sense of time matches the clock. Does that sound like a good plan?"

Ruby: *Barking with enthusiasm!*

The Great Escape

At Malmed Memorial, doctors developed diagnoses and treatment plans for patients and wrote orders directing nurses on how to care for their patients at bedside. The nurses, in turn, performed patient assessments, dispensed medications, treated wounds, took vital signs, charted patient and treatment data, and contacted doctors with questions or to alert them to a negative change in the patient's health. CNAs have a long string of duties, such as taking vital signs, bathing patients, changing the linens on their beds, feeding them, cleaning those who have soiled themselves, and helping with other activities of daily living, such as toileting, oral care, and grooming. And policing them, although that's not in the job description.

CNAs were either assigned to work the floor where they went room to room assisting patients, or they were ordered to "sit" with a patient for an entire shift. There are many reasons for doing so. For example, the patient may be a failed suicide planning a repeat attempt or someone with a high risk of falling who is confused and won't stay in bed.

To illustrate, I found myself sitting with an Ethiopian patient named Mr. Gedeyon who suffered from a variety of ailments, including mental illness, congestive heart failure, an injured leg, and kidney problems. When I say mentally ill, I'm referring to patients diagnosed as bipolar, schizophrenic, psychotic, or having a combination of these afflictions. We even had a patient, Maggie Peterson, who'd been diagnosed as a homicidal psychotic; she often ran through the hallways pursued by her CNA sitter on the days her doctor wouldn't sedate or restrain her. No assistant nurse could keep her in her room without getting attacked and injured.

As I sat with Mr. Gedeyon, he constantly yelled at doctors and nurses, fled his room, attempted to leave the hospital, and struck anyone who tried to impede his escape; he was fueled by manic energy. His doctors refused to sedate or restrain him. During the night, when managers were off duty and doctors were scarce, the nurses kept him in bed with humane soft wrist and ankle restraints. But every morning, his doctor ordered the restraints removed, commenting that they couldn't possibly be necessary.

"Let's see *you* sit with him, then," our nurses might say—in fantasy.

"Hey!" Mr. Gedeyon said to me. "I want to leave!"

"I'm sorry, Mr. Gedeyon," I said. "But your doctor wants you on bedrest. You're supposed to stay off your injured leg unless you need to use the bathroom."

"No!" he shouted.

Even though I sat in the doorway to his room with my computer, pretty much blocking it, he leaped out of bed and charged me like a well-muscled Olympic sprinter. Despite my size and strength, he banged past my left side and ran into the nurses' station, where about ten doctors, nurses, social workers, and clerks were conducting business, many of them on the phone.

"I want to leave!" he shouted. "I want to leave!"

"Get him under control!" a doctor barked at me.

This was the fourth time this scenario had played out that morning. I knew what would happen next. If I touched him in an attempt to steer him back to his room, he'd strike me.

"Get him under control, *now!*" the doctor yelled.

I put my hand on Mr. Gedeyon's shoulder and gently tried to turn him away from the nurses' station. In a flash, he punched me in my left shoulder, hard. Despite my training, it was all I could do not to smash my fist into him. Sometimes I could even put a name to this pent-up rage of mine: Dad. By this time, with the help of therapy, I'd become aware of how his violence had blighted my childhood, and that of my brother, Danny.

"Enough!" the charge nurse said; her name was Helen Adebayo, and she was a tall woman with a forceful personality. "If his doctors refuse to sedate or restrain him, they are the ones responsible for his behavior and safety. Allen, I release you from your duties. Let Mr. Gedeyon do whatever he likes."

Mr. Gedeyon ran through the nurses' station again; then he raced down the hall until he reached the elevators in the middle of our floor. He pushed the down button (leading to the lobby and exit), shouting and swinging his fists as nurses, doctors, and managers surrounded him to keep him on the floor. But there was nothing they

12

could do since there were no doctor orders to contain him.

Finally, a senior nurse named Sam Okonkwo said he'd take responsibility for Mr. Gedeyon. His strategy was to talk quietly with Mr. Gedeyon while allowing him to take in some fresh air just outside the hospital's main entrance, which would hopefully calm him and ease his claustrophobia.

As I later learned, as soon as Mr. Gedeyon saw the exit, he dashed for it like an NFL running back. In seconds, he was out the front door and up at street level, where he jumped onto a city bus a split second before it pulled away from the curb. He must have had correct change because the bus didn't stop.

Despite my limited experience at Malmed, I'd already detected certain patterns. *One more to fly the coup*, I thought.

Malmed Memorial had its own security force as well as a team of sheriff's deputies who were permanently assigned to the hospital. When Mr. Gedeyon ran through the lobby, Sam called out for Security to help him detain the patient, but they refused—patients are free to leave hospitals unless the police or a psychiatrist has placed them on a hold called a 5150 or a 5250, which means the patients are a danger to themselves or others and are legally forbidden from discharge. Mr. Gedeyon wasn't under any hold.

Shortly after Mr. Gedeyon fled the hospital, someone in management accused the nursing staff of encouraging him to leave. During the investigation, the nursing staff all told the same story: Mr. Gedeyon had legally discharged himself over our protests, and we'd been unable to control him because his doctor refused to order sedatives or restraints, a common occurrence at Malmed.

Incidents like this occurred frequently because our hospital didn't have a locked psychiatric unit, and most doctors appeared reluctant to order sedatives or restraints for these patients, including the combative ones. Our hospital was packed with mentally ill patients because it owned a separate psychiatric facility that sent us all patients who got injured or became ill there. In addition, many of our homeless patients had psychiatric issues. Nurses often fantasized about our hospital one day establishing a psych ward, not to mention a cafeteria. Ours had been moved to a distant building that housed clinics. It was virtually impossible to walk to the cafeteria, eat a meal, and return to the hospital during our thirty-minute meal breaks.

Mr. Gedeyon was the first patient to strike me, but he would be far from the last. When I examined my bruised shoulder that evening in the bathroom mirror, Elizabeth stared at the injury with shock that soon turned to outrage.

"How'd you get hurt?" she asked.

"A psych patient slugged me."

"And the hospital didn't do anything to protect you?"

"Nope."

"Is this going to be a common occurrence? Do I need to worry about you all the time like the spouse of a police officer?"

"I don't know," I said. "Let's see how it plays out."

Still shaking her head with anger and disbelief, Elizabeth brought me an ice pack wrapped in a towel and steered me to the couch, where she snuggled into me.

Mr. Gedeyon cycled through Malmed Memorial a few more times after his escape. I regret to report that Mr. Gedeyon eventually died in the hospital's care. According to his roommate, he entered their shared bathroom and never came out. A CNA discovered him two hours later slumped dead on the toilet when she came to take his vital signs. The hospital staff went to great lengths to revive him, but all attempts failed.

Usually, unexpected deaths are investigated by the coroner. Mr. Gedeyon's bed was visible from the nurses' station, and his RN was supposed to check on him as often as he could—this is a challenge, though, since each nurse on our floor cared for five patients, and some of them were time-consuming, total-care patients. The nurses were supposed to round with their patients hourly, but in a survey around that time, nurses said they were only able to round every two hours.

Shortly after Mr. Gedeyon died, I asked a senior nurse if she'd heard any scuttlebutt from the investigation.

She laughed. "What investigation?" she said. "The hospital decided Mr. Gedeyon was non-compliant in following medical instructions, and his death was his own fault. He died of too much fluid around his heart."

"And the hospital doesn't care about determining how we might prevent this situation from reoccurring in the future?" I said.

"Not a whit," she said.

Partners in Crime

Victor Chukwu, our unit's much-disliked director, once sent our homicidal psychotic patient, Maggie Peterson, to another hospital we owned, along with an assistant nurse, Yolanda Davis, to care for her. Yolanda was generally regarded as a low-rent assistant nurse— she was caught charting fake vital signs in the SDU unit, where patients were acutely ill or injured. This could have killed patients. Instead of getting fired, she was reassigned to work for Victor on our unit. She related the following story to me, which I believe, since it actually reflects badly on her as well as Victor.

"No matter how aggressively Maggie Peterson behaves," Victor told Yolanda, "don't chart it—I never want to see her again."

At the new hospital, Maggie Peterson attacked and injured several nurses, who all filed occurrence reports documenting violent patient behavior. When hospital investigators asked Yolanda why she hadn't done the same, she admitted she was under orders from Victor Chukwu not to chart such episodes. Despite the backlash this confession created, Victor was never punished, since he and his boss were close friends.

Horses in Sunlight

A good day at Malmed Memorial was any day that was not a bad day. Also, good days consisted of small but rewarding moments, such as making a patient laugh, cheering up a depressed person, and watching the worry disappear from someone's face when I explained a vital sign reading or a doctor's comment the individual had misinterpreted.

One of my favorite memories is working with a terminally ill patient named Mr. Shepherd, who was in a deep depression. A handsome middle-aged man, he was despondent because the hospital was trying to ship him to a nursing home to die while his dream was to spend his final days on a horse ranch owned by a close friend. The hospital was pushing hard for the nursing home, and Mr. Shepherd felt too sick and weak to fight for his dream.

But I convinced him to call his lawyer and the rancher friend and have *them* fight the hospital for him. This decision brightened his mood considerably.

"I *so* want to be on that ranch watching horses run in the sunshine," he said. Mr. Shepherd went on to say he'd written a letter of commendation for me and another nurse, which he'd submitted to Victor Chukwu. I thanked him, pretending I knew all about it. Victor was notorious for not passing along patient praise to staff, which is one of the many reasons we called him Fuck You Chuck behind his back.

A couple of days later, I met the horse rancher friend and shook Mr. Shepherd's hand as EMTs gently transferred him onto the gurney that would be his bed while he rode in the ambulance up to the ranch.

Frequent Flyers

The day after I said goodbye to Mr. Shepherd, I sat with an elderly man named Mr. Brown, who was mentally ill and recovering from a broken hip. My mission was to keep him in bed. After lying quiet and lucid for about five minutes, he would suddenly leap out of bed and lunge toward the door leading to the hallway. As soon as he put weight on his bad hip, he would cry out and start to fall. So we developed a little dance. Every time he tried to stand up, I gently pushed him back down into the bed and held him there for about a minute until his mind cleared and he calmed. This cycle repeated itself for the rest of the day.

At one point, he suddenly jumped out of bed with an extra burst of confused energy and made his strongest attempt yet to leave his room.

"Let me out of here, you goddamn son of a bitch!" he snarled.

"Mr. Brown, your doctor doesn't want you walking with that injured hip," I said.

As I gently wrestled with him to prevent him from falling while also steering him back to bed, he shouted, "Get your fuckin' hands off me!"

He punched me in the chest. Ripples and echoes. Boy, did I want to clock him!

"You will *not* hit me!" I yelled, finally forcing him back into bed and holding him down until he relaxed again.

Of course, I shouldn't have raised my voice. Nurses aren't allowed to verbally or physically abuse their patients—we can lose our licenses for this, and justifiably so. FYI—CNA schools drill into our brains all the offenses that could cause us to lose our licenses.

"Allen, you okay in there?" a nurse named Renee Patterson called from the hallway.

"Yes," I said. I felt comforted that my colleague would have provided immediate assistance if I'd needed it.

17

While Mr. Brown went through his latest five-minute calm period, I wondered again why his doctor refused to sedate or restrain him—we had special medications to relax mentally ill patients, and, although I'm not a doctor, I didn't see any contraindications for the use of such drugs. Also, Mr. Brown had regularly stayed with us, and he'd always been volatile and aggressive. One would've thought his doctors would have learned that by then.

We referred to patients like Mr. Brown, who repeatedly cycled through the hospital, as "frequent flyers." This term also encompassed the working stiffs such as yours truly roaming the halls day after day, year after year. Within the hospital, this was a universally recognized term.

In addition, I've invented a few other categories of patients, such as one-timers—patients who want to get well and go home; Houdinis—people who continually try to escape, despite the severity of their illnesses and injuries; and burrowers—patients who want to stay in the hospital for the rest of their lives, even though they may be healed and perfectly healthy.

Later that day, Mr. Brown's wife came to visit. She seemed a bit eccentric herself, but functional. Usually, when a family came to visit a "sitter patient," the CNA sitter was allowed to take a break or shift to working the floor, since the family had unofficially taken over the sitter's responsibilities. However, shortly after Mr. Brown's wife arrived, his nurse, Beza, took me aside and instructed me not to give up my post, since the patient was crazed, assaultive, and likely to fall. Just as Beza walked away, Mary Savage, our unit's assistant manager, told me to work the floor for the remainder of my shift.

"I'm not sure what to do," I said. "Beza just told me to stay with Mr. Brown. Do you want to coordinate with her?"

Mary Savage was an imposing woman with a hair-trigger temper. "Are you out of your *mind*?" she said. "I'm your boss, and when I tell you to do something, you *do* it, *now*! Is that clear?"

I traded Mr. Brown for floor duty.

At the end of my shift, I sought out Mary to smooth things over. "I'm sorry about earlier," I said. "I've never been given conflicting instructions before, so I didn't quite know what to do."

Mary lost her temper again. "I can't believe the blatant insubordination you showed me! I *never* need to coordinate with *anyone*. I'm your boss, and when I give you an order, you *follow* it!"

"I understand," I said.

"That old man's a disaster waiting to happen," she said. "His wife's going to have to watch him every second at home—she might as well get used to it now."

I didn't point out that patient safety was the hospital's responsibility as long as the patients were in our care. And I tried my best to hide the anxiety her scolding had induced.

When I described this incident to my therapist, Ginger Lightfoot, a few days later, she said, "I think your PTSD journey is going to be a rocky road as long as you're working for Malmed Memorial and experiencing screaming nurses and violent patients. These incidents will exacerbate your PTSD and set you back. However, we're doing good work together, and you're also on an internal, healing path that has nothing to do with what's happening at work."

Man Down

After a gray blur of uneventful days, we admitted a patient named Bill Wilkinson, who'd shattered his leg in a motorcycle accident. He was in agonizing pain. He taught me how to hold his injured leg so he could transfer himself from his bed onto the bedside commode with a minimum of suffering. He always called for me when he needed this task performed. Despite his serious condition, he exhibited an outstanding sense of humor, which was dampened only when he received truly upsetting news, such as that some of the blood clots that had formed in his injured leg had migrated to his lungs, which could prove fatal. I caught him crying after that diagnosis, but I held back at the door, so he didn't see me.

Bill's wife, Susan, constantly sat at his bedside. Although angry with him for not giving up his motorcycle riding after his previous accident, she treated him with loving-kindness. I became close to both of them, especially Bill. I checked on him frequently to keep him comfortable.

Once when I visited him, he spiked a fever of 105, his body drenched in sweat. The rest of his vital signs displayed alarming values, as if his body had suddenly gone haywire. This condition lasted twenty-four hours, and I worried for the first time that Bill might die—I had no idea a shattered leg could prove fatal. Luckily, Bill knew his body, ordering his doctors to take him off all medications, except for his antibiotic. They complied. He endured tremendous pain and risked the blood clots in his lungs killing him. Within a few hours, Bill's health returned to normal, and his doctors discharged him a couple of days later.

We happened to share the same primary doctor—we've bumped into each other several times in the waiting room. We're always delighted to see each other.

"Thanks for saving my life," he frequently says.

Hell-Hole Room

Shortly after Bill left the hospital, I sat in what I call a "hell-hole" room, a chamber in which a single assistant nurse oversees the care and control of four patients—almost always the four most difficult people on the unit, such as mentally ill and hostile patients who lack sedation and restraints. These areas presented a danger to both patients and nurses. Two of our senior nurses had asked our nursing manager, Rose Oni, to eliminate these rooms, and she seemed sympathetic, but our nursing director, Victor Chukwu, created these spaces to save money on assistant nurse labor costs, and he refused to budge on the issue.

When I entered the room, a team of doctors and a nurse stood by the bed of a patient named Mr. Stevens, who wore a serious-looking oxygen mask and slept deeply.

The lead doctor said, "Allen, we need you to watch this patient carefully. First, do not let him take off his oxygen mask or even knock it askew because he will desat quickly." (Lose the high oxygen saturation in his blood required for stable health.) "Second, Mr. Stevens has a broken bone in his back. Do not under any circumstances let him thrash in bed or try to sit up because he could permanently paralyze himself. Right now, he's heavily sedated, but we're letting the sedative wear off. The instant he stirs, notify his nurse. She'll have to put him in a back brace before he can sit up."

I nodded my understanding.

As soon as the nurse and medical team left, I took stock of my other three patients. Patient 2: Mr. Anderson, an elderly man withdrawing from alcohol. Delirious, he'd broken his left collar bone in a drunken fall at home.

Patient 3: a mentally ill man in sheriff's custody who alternated curses, screams, and a nonsense song about selling fruits and candies. Two deputies had handcuffed him by his wrists and ankles to his bed and stood watch.

Patient 4: Mr. Schneider, a confused elderly man with a tumor the size of a small watermelon on the right side of his neck. Disoriented and unsteady on his feet, he needed help walking to the bathroom so he wouldn't fall.

The instant I finished this quick inventory, Mr. Anderson, the delirious patient with the broken collar bone, leaped out of his bed and barreled unsteadily across the room toward the door.

"Mr. Anderson," I said. "Your doctors want you to stay in bed. Can you come back, please?"

"I have to pick up my kids from school," he said.

Given his advanced age, it was unlikely he had young children.

As he shot out into the hall, I followed, stress level skyrocketing.

As much as I wanted to watch Mr. Stevens, I believed Mr. Anderson was in more imminent danger—he could fall, re-break his collar bone, hit his head, or sustain other serious injuries, while Mr. Stevens remained in a deep sleep. Also, hopefully, Mr. Schneider wouldn't get up to use the bathroom while we were gone. If any harm came to these patients while I chased Mr. Anderson, I could've lost my license. On the other hand, if I'd let Mr. Anderson run out of the room without me and he fell and injured himself, I also might've lost my license.

Every time I tried to steer Mr. Anderson back to his room, he swung a fist at my face. At one point, I dragged him out of an elevator car; he went in the open door as we'd passed.

"Let go of me, you son of a bitch! I have to pick up my kids from school! I can't leave them on the street!"

For his safety, I tried to manipulate Mr. Anderson using his delusion. "Mr. Anderson, don't you remember, there's no school today. Your kids are at home with your wife."

"Bullshit!" he shouted.

"Oh, I remember now. Your wife called and said she'd pick up the kids today so you can rest in bed and get better."

"Lies!" he bellowed. "Mendacity!"

As the minutes passed with me trailing him to prevent or break his fall, I felt increasingly anxious about Mr. Stevens and Mr. Schneider. It was only a matter of time before one or both of them injured themselves from lack of supervision.

Just then, we met charge nurse Carmen Sanchez in the hall. I quickly explained my predicament and asked for her help.

"You stay with Mr. Anderson," she said. She did not comment on how she was going to protect the other two patients in my room, who weren't handcuffed, from harming themselves. Carmen lived in fear of Victor, and her sole mission was to avoid his wrath.

I followed Mr. Anderson all over the floor and wrestled him away from open elevator doors for hours. When he finally tired and returned to his bed, I saw that Mr. Stevens had been removed to the

Step-Down Unit or SDU. In our hospital, the most acutely ill and injured patients resided in the Intensive Care Unit or ICU. When their conditions stabilized, they were moved to the SDU. Mr. Steven's transfer meant that either his condition had worsened, or his doctors and nurse had placed him there for more careful monitoring. I fervently hoped he hadn't taken a turn for the worse on my watch.

Carmen hadn't assigned an assistant nurse to sit in my room in my absence. Good thing "patient safety" was the hospital's primary concern. Maybe when the executives muttered their patient safety mantra, they believed an invisible force field magically enveloped the facility, protecting all unattended high-fall-risk patients from harm.

I assisted Mr. Schneider to the bathroom. As soon as I got him back to bed, a deputy sheriff handed a hot cup of coffee to his prisoner. Despite his handcuffs, the patient threw the hot coffee all over Mr. Schneider, who shrieked.

Just then, Mr. Anderson bolted with a wobbly gait out the door again. I followed. While I chased Mr. Anderson, I flagged down an assistant nurse and asked her to please check Mr. Schneider for burns and help him get clean and dry. Then I pursued Mr. Anderson for the rest of my shift.

As I surveyed my hell-hole room shortly before I punched out, Mr. Anderson having tired and returned to his bed, I was joined by Jack (short for Jaqueline), a beloved senior nurse on our unit who emanated warmth and compassion that caused most of us to love and trust her. She'd seen me chasing Mr. Anderson all over our unit, and she knew that I'd been in an untenable situation in the hell-hole room all day.

We discussed how much we hated hell-hole rooms, and Jack told me she'd lost two bitter arguments with Victor Chukwu about eliminating them. As a result, she was thinking about reporting Victor and the hell-hole rooms to the California Department of Public Health, an action I was also considering, especially since one could complain anonymously.

Moved by this moment of solidarity, I patted Jack's shoulder.

As soon as I touched her, she slid her arm around my shoulders, and I did the same with her. I don't have any childhood memories of feeling comforted while snuggled in my mother's arms. Ginger Lightfoot, my therapist, has suggested this never happened, which is why I have trouble feeling safe and calm when stressed. So Jack's touch felt wonderful. We held the sideways hug just long enough to reassure ourselves that we were fellow good guys fighting the forces of evil.

Touch

Toward the end of my shift sitting in another four-patient hell-hole room, I'd managed to get all of my patients to take a nap or rest quietly. I was stationed at the foot of the bed of an elderly Chinese man dying from lung cancer. He was attended by his wife, who was speaking to his tall Middle Eastern doctor via a translator telephone. I could hear only the doctor's side of the conversation. It became clear the grieving wife understood her husband could die at any moment, but she was imploring the doctor to keep her husband alive for a few more days so their grown children, who lived overseas, would have time to visit him and say goodbye.

"I promise we'll keep your husband as comfortable as possible," the doctor said. "But I can't control the timing of his death. Hopefully, he can hang on long enough to see your children, but there are no guarantees. I'm really sorry. I wish I could do more."

When the wife realized her husband might die without seeing their children, she became inconsolable, sobbing into her delicate hands, which hid her face.

Touch her, I mentally signaled to the doctor, and he did just that. He put his long arm around her tiny shoulders and held her until she calmed.

After the doctor left and it was time for me to punch out, I checked Mr. Cheng carefully to make sure he was clean, dry, and comfortable.

"Thank you," his wife said, bowing.

"You're welcome," I said. "I'm sorry your husband's so sick, but he's comfortable." I returned her small bow. I knew she couldn't understand me, but I was pretty sure my expression told her all she needed to know. Then I patted her on the shoulder, saying goodbye. I was surprised when she threw her arms around me and wept into my chest, but I held her, just as the doctor had done, until her tears slowed, and she reluctantly pulled away.

World-Class Customer Service—NOT!

I heard crying coming from a patient's room.

"Hello?" I said, peering inside.

Sitting on a bedside commode was an elderly African American man. He trembled with cold and fatigue, and tears streamed down his face.

"Please help me," he said. "I'm an old man, and I can't walk anymore. My nurse put me on this toilet, then forgot about me. I've been calling out for help for the last hour, but no one's come."

I noticed Mr. Wilson's nurse had failed to leave his call light button within reach, a major mistake. Also, she should have circled back to check on him about ten minutes after she transferred him onto the commode.

"I'll help you right now," I said.

"Oh, God bless you, honey," he said. "I feel like a little boy being toilet trained. I'm stuck here alone, and I can't even stand up and wipe my ass. And this seat is really uncomfortable—it's killing the backs of my legs. And I'm freezing."

I helped Mr. Wilson to his feet, wiped his bottom with a warm washcloth, and transferred him back into bed. After I got him comfortable under a pile of our red-pink hospital blankets, I noticed his weeping hadn't abated.

"This is the most humiliated I've been in my adult life," he said in a tremulous voice. "My nurse doesn't even treat me like I'm a human being. This is inexcusable! I'd like to talk to the head nurse about this. Could you please arrange that?"

"Yes, sir," I said. "Our charge nurse is Sam Okonkwo. I'll have him come see you as soon as he can." I liked Sam and felt assured he'd lend Mr. Wilson a sympathetic ear and take any required follow-up actions, such as speaking with Mr. Wilson's nurse.

Sam was charting at the main nurses' station. When I related what had happened, he frowned and said, "Thanks for telling me. That's unfortunate. I'll be happy to speak with Mr. Wilson."

I felt a wave of relief, but it gradually vanished, because I worked near the nurses' station for the rest of my shift, and Sam never left it.

Diamond in the Rough

I disliked Mr. Perry's foul temper, which I feared might lead to violence. Nevertheless, I entered his room to check on him.

Mr. Perry was about sixty with breathing issues. He constantly complained that his coffee was cold, or he didn't like his meal, or why had the kitchen put milk on his tray when he was lactose intolerant? Nurses were not involved in food preparation, although we did double-check patient meal trays and try to prevent sugary items from being served to diabetics and so forth. I was wary of Mr. Perry, but I tried to meet his needs the best I could. I speculated maybe he was a cranky bus driver who'd damaged his lungs from too much smoking. I imagined him sitting at home drinking beer and smoking in front of a small television, shouting at his favorite team's ball players who blew plays.

Then one day I caught him in a peaceful mood. He was reading something on his iPhone.

"Remember those pamphlets you could buy that told you all the main points of a book you were supposed to read for high school but didn't?" he said.

"Cliff Notes?" I said.

"Yeah, that's it—Cliff Notes! Well, now there's tons of stuff like that for free on the internet. I'm reading through the works of Shakespeare—right now I'm on *The Taming of the Shrew*. Shakespeare expresses himself so beautifully with words, but I don't understand the outdated ones, so I look up the plot of each play and the Elizabethan words that have gone out of use. That way, I get the full experience." He smiled.

I thought about the way Shakespeare enjoyed playing with appearance versus reality, such as having Rosalind disguise herself as a man in *As You Like It*. Even though my CNA position required only a high school diploma, I was glad my college degrees allowed me to connect with patients such as Mr. Perry. I realized now he masqueraded as a curmudgeon while possessing a poet's heart.

Fuck You Chuck Fucks Up

Soon after my Shakespeare conversation with Mr. Perry, charge nurse, Beza, assigned me to a single-patient sitter room. The patient was Mr. Gibson, another one of our frequent flyers. He was mentally ill and drank alcohol in large quantities to self-medicate, so when we dried him out, his mental illness and his violent urges rose to the surface. When I entered his room, he bucked in his bed like a wounded animal, struggling against his wrist and ankle restraints. He screamed and cursed, clearly addressing people who were hallucinations.

"Mr. Gibson," I said. "If you calm down and relax, we can remove your restraints later on today, but you have to be good." In general, this was true, although I knew no one in their right mind would remove his restraints *that* day.

Mr. Gibson showed no signs he'd seen or heard me. He continued to curse and thrash and shriek at imaginary people.

I addressed him again, but he remained oblivious to my presence. *Thank God he's restrained*, I thought. Mr. Gibson was a bull of a man in his prime and could seriously injure someone without much effort. I marveled at the way he'd transformed from a mellow drunk into a Hulked-out rage monster, similar to the way my slight and unassuming father could explode with sudden fury during my childhood, a real Jekyll and Hyde act.

A few minutes later, an assistant nurse named Tanya stopped in the doorway and said, "Beza has a task for you. Go see her, and I'll sit here until you come back."

So I left and reported to Beza. She asked me to take some extra vital signs on behalf of an assistant nurse who was running late.

Later, Tanya told me that right after I left the room, our director of nursing, Fuck You Chuck, talked to Mr. Gibson's nurse, Renee Patterson, right outside his room.

"Remove his restraints," he said.

Renee stared at him, incredulous. "But sir, I don't understand," she said. "The patient's hallucinating and combative right now."

"Release him," he said. "He doesn't need a sitter *and* restraints."

"But he's likely to hurt someone," she said. "Can't we remove the sitter and keep the restraints, since we can watch him from the nurses' station and hall?"

Victor lost his temper. "Listen, Renee, I'll be frank with you. I have no confidence you'll properly document his restraints, and I don't want to get in trouble with the state (department of public health). I've made my decision, now carry it out!"

He stormed off, which is typical. Fuck You Chuck had a habit of fleeing just before the disastrous consequences of one of his bone-headed decisions became apparent. And, for the record, Renee was a skilled RN who frequently served as our charge nurse, and she certainly knew how to chart patient restraints.

While I was taking vital signs, Tanya suddenly cried out for help. She called out twice more, but nobody ran to assist her, so I sprinted toward Mr. Gibson's room. When I got there, Mr. Gibson was unrestrained and thrashing wildly on the bed while Tanya pressed on his chest with one hand to keep him down while trying to fend off his floundering arms with her other hand. I put both hands on Mr. Gibson's chest and pressed down, hard. Fortunately for us, Mr. Gibson had temporarily lost some motor control in his arms, so he couldn't punch us, but this didn't stop him from grabbing Tanya's right arm and pinching it so viciously she screamed and began to cry.

"I'll take over," I said. "You get help, and have your arm looked at."

Tanya fled the room.

I held Mr. Gibson down for nearly an hour.

At one point, Beza looked into the room. "Please get help," I said. "This guy needs sedation, restraints, or both." Since Victor had forbidden restraints, I knew she'd have to get a doctor's order to sedate the patient, unless there was a previous order still in effect.

Later on, the assistant manager of our unit, Mary Savage, appeared in the doorway.

"I'm giving you fair warning," I said. "If this problem doesn't get resolved soon, I'm letting go!"

Nothing happened for long minutes. Mr. Gibson continued his wild bucking and repeatedly attempted to kick me and scratch or pinch my arms. The room stank of sweat and body odor.

Finally, and I have no idea how I accomplished this, I called my former boss at the hospital, Rick Sanford, using one hand and the speed dial on my cell phone. When I was unable to reach him, I left a desperate message.

Still, nothing happened.

Finally, at the end of the hour, Beza and a burly physical therapist named Roxanne came into the room and watched us. I was fatigued and angry.

"I'm letting go in three seconds!" I shouted.

I counted and let go.

Roxanne immediately pinned Mr. Gibson to the bed while Beza reapplied his restraints. Why couldn't someone have done that much earlier? Because only *I* was in danger, not a doctor or RN. In fact, Tanya told me later that when she called out for help, the RNs near her room ran and hid around a corner. I didn't witness this, so I can't testify whether it's true, but it probably is, since I'm the only one who came when Tanya cried out for assistance.

A few weeks before this, our union placed a poster on the wall of our floor that talked about the union's efforts to reduce violence against nurses. This announcement described an incident at our hospital in which a doctor used a female assistant nurse as a human shield against an assaultive patient.

Later that day, Rose Oni came to me and asked me to fill out an occurrence report for submission to Risk Management. She indicated this was necessary because she wanted that department to know about Victor's rash decision, which he was still defending. I agreed and did so.

Then it occurred to me that Rose lacked the courage to report him herself.

As soon as I returned home, I called in sick for the next day and drank pinot noir with a sympathetic Elizabeth until the world was once again a fine and mellow place.

Morale on our unit was so low that whenever I came upon a cluster of nurses I respected, they were almost always sharing tips about which local good-reputation hospitals were seeking RNs. One of my assistant nurse colleagues was so desperate to get away from Victor and the hell-hole rooms that she gave up patient care and became a morgue attendant!

Victor's latest stunt so disgusted me that I began what would be a three-year fruitless effort to change hospitals. Apparently, I didn't have enough experience yet to jump to another facility. Also, hospitals don't like hiring new workers as full-time employees.

Instead, they prefer to engage new people as per diem employees who work eight days a month without benefits. After three or four months, hospitals bring the high performers onboard full time. Based on my experience, Malmed's version of this technique was to allow new employees to work full-time without benefits for several years before they were permitted to become full-time benefitted employees. By contrast, Kaiser offered new employees thirteen-week contracts without any guarantee of renewal. In short, employees with full-time jobs bear all the risk when attempting to change hospitals.

My wife, Elizabeth, fully supported my decision to job hunt because she wanted me to be happy and safe at work. However, she told me later she secretly hoped I could learn to tolerate Malmed so I could continue to enjoy high pay and obtain a full-time permanent position with excellent benefits and a pension plan. Our salaries covered our basic needs, but we couldn't afford any extra expenses, even anticipated ones, such as renewing our car registrations.

In fact, Elizabeth lives in terror of us not having enough money to stay afloat. In the early days of our relationship, she struggled as a working single mom to make ends meet. One week, she encountered an unforeseen expense that left her unable to buy food. We concluded a weekend together with me paying for a week's groceries.

Later on, we were flush; then I faced two years of unemployment—when I returned to work, my salary as a swimming coach and teacher comprised only a small fraction of the executive-level income to which we'd been accustomed. So life taught her that having an adequate amount of money is a roller coaster ride that can plunge into the red at any moment. Presently, we can pay our bills, but we live from paycheck to paycheck, like so many other Americans.

Déjà vu All Over Again

Shortly after Victor unleashed Mr. Gibson on his staff, we were invited to tour the nearly completed new hospital that would replace our current building, which was slated for demolition. Several nurses and I attended orientation and training in the new facility, which looked like a five-star hotel and was equipped with all-new medical equipment. At first, the walk-through was exciting, but as we finished our nine-floor tour, our group grumbled.

"What is it?" asked our puzzled tour guide, a well-liked manager.

"So where's the cafeteria?" a nurse demanded.

The manager blushed. "I'm sorry," he said. "But the hospital planners didn't think we needed one."

"Screw the cafeteria," said an angry African American nurse in her sixties. "Where the hell's the psych ward?"

The manager turned even more crimson. "Sorry," he said. "Same answer."

Flight Two: 2015

Zodiac Dreams

A Would-be Rocky

The doctor fucked up, and Deshawn Johnson punched eight nurses, including yours truly, and sent us to the emergency room in our new facility before we successfully pressured his physician into prescribing a sedative to pacify him. Deshawn was schizophrenic and wildly violent. He attacked anyone with whom he came in contact. He first entered our hospital via the emergency room. He'd been living on the street until he assaulted another homeless man, who defended himself by stabbing Deshawn twice in the chest. He was treated and transferred to the intensive care unit.

When he tried to strike the ICU nurses, his doctor prescribed a sedative called Versed or midazolam, which is very strong and potentially can stop the heart or lungs. Patients taking this medication must be on heart and lung monitors, which are present in the ICU.

When Deshawn's condition improved and he was transferred to our medical-surgical unit, which lacks heart and lung monitors, his doctor neglected to prescribe an appropriate new sedative. As a result, our would-be Rocky swung and connected with eight nurses, despite the fact that he was bound by humane soft medical wrist and ankle restraints.

Here's how he hit me. When I entered his room, he was eating breakfast with metal silverware, his right hand unrestrained. That's two fuckups right there. He should have been fed by me with plastic silverware while he was fully restrained.

I introduced myself, told him I was going to spend the day in his room to help him with his needs, and then sat quietly in a chair while he finished breakfast.

"I gotta use the bathroom," he said.

"I'm sorry, but your doctors want you on complete bedrest. You shouldn't have to pee because you have a Foley catheter that's draining your bladder," I said. No way was I going to let this angry and combative patient have the use of all four limbs.

"I need to take a shit, you dumb mother-fucker, and I want to do it now, in the bathroom!" he shouted.

"In that case, I'll get you a bed pan," I said.

"Fuck the bed pan!" he yelled. "I'm using the bathroom, now!"

With his free right hand, he reached to release his left wrist. Grabbing the loose restraint, I tried to snap it back in place, but he jerked it away, and then backhanded me in the face, hard. My glasses flew off, and I staggered backward. Then I caught and held tight to the untethered restraint, calling out for help. We played an intense game of tug-of-war. I didn't want him to free his left hand or snatch up the metal knife on his breakfast tray.

The patient's primary nurse, Helen Adebayo, arrived almost immediately and told me to let go of the restraint and step out of the room. At the same time, she asked a nurse to activate a Code Gray, which means violent person. Within a few minutes, two county sheriff's deputies rushed into Deshawn's room with a nurse and reapplied his restraint. I was sent to the emergency room. My face hurt, I was angry at the bozo who'd removed Deshawn's restraint and allowed him to have metal silverware, I was livid at Deshawn for striking me, I was pissed off at the doctor who failed to sedate him, and I was suddenly—unexpectedly—furious with my father.

"Would you like to press charges now?" asked the deputy who

escorted me to the emergency room.

"No, I don't think so," I said. "He's mentally ill and can't help himself."

"Yeah, but you're the seventh nurse he's punched so far, and I think the D.A. needs to know how violent this guy is."

So I ended up pressing charges, but the D.A. threw out the case, deciding to prosecute Deshawn for a more serious crime instead.

After Deshawn had been clobbering nurses for two weeks, his doctor finally put him on two milligrams of Ativan, which kept him peaceful for the rest of his stay.

When I came home after work on the day Deshawn slugged me, my anger had become laser-focused on Malmed Memorial. It was clear the union claims about the hospital not giving a damn about staff safety were true. So far, I'd been punched in the shoulder, struck in the chest, and hit in the face by out-of-control, combative psych patients. In addition, I'd witnessed the aftermath of our director, Victor Chukwu, forcing Renee Patterson to release the hallucinating and violent Mr. Gibson, and I'd experienced the chaos and danger represented by four-patient hell-hole rooms.

I once read the secret to a successful marriage is for each partner to try their best to be the person their spouse most needs them to be, and I've attempted to follow that rule ever since. Clearly, Elizabeth was most comfortable with me holding a highly secure job with high pay and comprehensive benefits. On the other hand, she loved me and hated to see me hurt.

When I'd been in the emergency room waiting to have my face examined, I'd texted her about Deshawn's assault. Upon arriving home that evening, Elizabeth rushed to embrace me and then pulled back to examine my injuries (cuts where my glasses had been driven into my face), her blue eyes filled with concern.

"The day is coming," I said. "When we might have to choose between high pay and job security and my personal safety. I know you worry a lot about money, but I'm hoping we'll both come down on the right side of that decision."

"I'm sorry I worry about it so much," she said. "But I'll always choose your safety." And I knew she spoke the truth.

Elizabeth hugged me even tighter, as if I were filled with helium, like one of my patient's get-well-soon Mylar balloons, and she was afraid I'd fly away.

Camp Runamuk

Violence was common in our hospital, and we assistant nurses got the worst of it because we had the most patient contact. Once, a mentally ill female patient leaped out of bed, knocked a CNA named Martha down, grabbed her by the hair, and repeatedly smashed her head against the floor. The charge nurse, Violet, happened to be in the room. She made no effort to intervene. Instead, she left the room and activated a Code Gray. I lost all respect for Violet, and Martha, who was seriously injured, hated her. I later read in a union flyer that Martha sustained permanent injuries during that assault.

Something similar happened to me. A mentally ill patient without restraints or sedation got out of bed and faked a fall. When I helped him to his feet, he grabbed me by the balls. This patient later attacked a doctor with a metal knife he wasn't supposed to have because the dietary staff or his nurse or his doctor fucked up about the silverware, and his doctor refused to sedate or restrain him. Doctors and nurses with combative/suicidal patients were supposed to tell the kitchen staff to provide plastic rather than metal silverware with meals, but they rarely did so. Also, kitchen/dietary staff members didn't always comply with these orders.

Here's the kicker. We were not a mental hospital—we were a county general hospital. Unfortunately for the assistant nurses, our parent company owned a psychiatric facility, and whenever the patients there became sick or injured, they were transferred to our hospital. And many of our homeless patients were mentally ill.

Whenever one of us was hurt by a patient, we said to each other,

"Welcome to Malmed Memorial!"

And a Code Gray is not the most dangerous code. A Code Silver indicates a patient or visitor is armed with a weapon, and a Code 10 denotes an active shootout outside of the emergency room entrance.

Hitman

Psychiatric patients didn't present the only danger to nurses. Occasionally, a hitman would wander our halls seeking to finish off a patient who was shot on the street but not killed. We once had a patient who ratted out his best friend's illegal operation (I don't know what it was) to the police. Furious, the betrayed friend blasted the informant with a shotgun, but he aimed too low, hitting him in the legs. We kept this patient under a false name and put him in a bed surrounded by curtains and far from the door of his two-patient room.

Despite these precautions, the shooter called this patient on his room phone and said, "Just thought you'd like to know I'm sending someone to finish the job."

The patient immediately reported this call, and further efforts were made regarding his safekeeping. A few hours later, an alert nurse noticed a man carrying a shoulder bag that probably concealed a gun walking from room to room, peering in at each patient. He wasn't wearing a visitor identification badge. When she confronted him, he fled. She called Security and the sheriff's deputies, but the man escaped. The hitman was a short, white guy with black hair who needed a shave. When he was searching for his victim, I was sitting with a patient, and he looked directly at me with his cold fisheyes.

Searching for Safety

Shortly after the hitman scare, a patient on the floor below us created a commotion by brandishing a loaded gun. Our hospital didn't employ metal detectors and often failed to check patient belongings for dangerous contraband. Some patients smuggled in weapons, needles, and drugs, such as heroin, that they shot into their IV ports while in their bathrooms. Also, despite the frequent presence of weapons, our unit's live-shooter training at this point consisted of a one-hour video played once during a lightly attended 6:00 a.m. staff meeting.

In addition, our facility was supposed to provide a self-defense class called Combative Patient Intervention with annual refresher courses. I took the live course when I first came onboard, but it was discontinued. To replace it, the hospital released an e-learning class about dealing with aggressive patients, but the self-defense aspect, which was four hours long in the in-person class, was barely addressed—the sole message was to push assaultive patients away from you, step back, and call for help; there was no advice, say, on how to escape from a stranglehold or from a patient who's grabbed you by the hair and is trying to break your neck.

Since Malmed was a major regional trauma center, the hospital was packed with inner-city gang members in their teens and twenties who came in with one or more gunshot wounds. A few of these patients were grateful to us for patching them up, but most were pissed off they'd been shot, and took their fury out on the staff, even though they liked to brag to their friends about "taking a bullet."

If you startled male gang member patients while they were sleeping, such as gently touching their arms or shoulders to wake them for vital signs, they often lashed out with a fist. And they may have possessed weapons. So I developed this simple rule: if I stood outside of a patient's reach and couldn't wake him by loudly speaking his name, I let him sleep. This is an extension of something

40

I learned from painful experiences as a child: if my father was in a room at home, I avoided it. Both situations clutched my throat. Despite my weekly therapy, the constant threat of physical harm at Malmed aggravated my PTSD.

Pariah

On average, though, many of our patients were friendly and appreciated our care, and they were a pleasure to serve. Sometimes we became really close to them. For example, I sat with Robert almost every day for a couple of weeks. He had long, black hair and thick glasses. He used to be a math and science professor at UC Berkeley but eventually lost this job, perhaps because he was schizophrenic. In any event, when he came to our hospital, he had difficultly moving his right arm and leg. At first, his doctors thought he was afflicted with catatonia, a psychiatric condition in which a patient loses the ability to move part or all of his body, but they later determined he suffered from the onset of Parkinson's disease, a degenerative condition with no cure.

Robert spent a lot of time sleeping, but when he was awake, I fed him his meals (it took him an hour to eat), helped him brush his teeth, changed him if he was wet or soiled, assisted him with bed baths, and repositioned him every two hours so he remained comfortable and avoided bed sores. Robert liked to chat, joke, and present me with math puzzles to solve. We were both sixty, so we'd passed through the same periods of American history, which we discussed. We became friends.

Then one day Carmen decided Robert didn't require a CNA to sit with him because he wasn't a danger to himself or others, and he wasn't a fall risk because he could not get out of bed. This was a valid and logical decision, but it triggered a sad turn of events. Robert became a pariah because none of the RNs or assistant nurses had much time to spare for him. RNs cared for five patients, while assistant nurses cared for nine to twenty-eight, depending on staffing levels.

CNAs ensured patients received baths or showers, fresh linens on their beds, ice water, a clean room, meals (including feeding total care patients), and anything else they might reasonably request. We also alerted the RNs when these patients required pain meds or other services that could only be provided by an RN, such as the repair of a leaking IV. These duties required an entire shift to complete.

Suddenly no one had time to feed Robert for an hour or spend fifteen minutes repositioning him until he finally felt comfortable. And, as it turned out, Robert was highly anxious about being left alone, so he repeatedly called out for help. When an RN or assistant nurse checked on him, he would make up a list of needs to keep the nurse in his room for as long as possible—it became difficult to enter his room without losing up to an hour.

One day I came to work to discover Robert had been transferred to another healthcare facility. But I still think of him and feel bad that he flip-flopped from a beloved patient to a persona non grata.

Zodiac Dreams

So what did it take for a CNA to have a good day at Malmed Memorial? First, we needed a friendly charge nurse since several of them treated CNAs with tremendous disdain. Second, we required hard-working nurses who utilized us only when truly necessary, and, finally, we needed a set of reasonable patients. For all three conditions to occur on the same day was like a perfect planetary alignment that happens once every thousand years!

Let's meet a couple of the less desirable charge nurses. Carmen Sanchez was terrified she'd get in trouble with management if the staff failed to perform properly. Therefore, she wandered the halls chastising staff members, especially assistant nurses, telling us how to do our jobs. Most of the time, she misread the tasks we were performing and scolded us about steps she incorrectly thought we'd failed to do or had done wrong.

Early in my career at Malmed, I had a major run-in with Carmen. Day shift assistant nurses took vital signs at 11:00 a.m. Often at this time, we were sitting with particularly ill, injured, or endangered patients, and weren't allowed to exit the room unless someone replaced us. If we left these patients alone and something bad happened to them, we could lose our licenses.

At 11:00 a.m., the nurse for whom we were sitting was supposed to relieve us, but this rarely happened. My colleagues solved this problem by abandoning their patients, wandering the halls, and visiting the nurses' stations until they found a nurse who agreed to break them.

This approach achieved the desired results, but it put patients at risk, which I refused to do. So I sat in my assigned room and, assuming I had access to a phone, called my patient's nurse, asking her to please relieve me. Many said they were too busy, even though we were doing them a favor by taking vital signs for them. So Carmen chewed me out for not showing initiative in getting an RN to sit for me.

"I can't abandon my patient," I explained. "I can't force a busy RN to break me. And I don't always have a phone in my sitter rooms." Carmen didn't buy it.

Later that day, Carmen criticized me in my assigned room and then later sat down next to me in the break room and upbraided me while I ate my lunch. Since the break room was a sanctuary, several RNs persuaded Carmen to leave me alone. After lunch, I reported Carmen to our nursing manager, Rose Oni, who confirmed my behavior was correct. Carmen denied scolding me, but she was at it again two weeks later.

However, Carmen was an ideal charge nurse compared to Aretta Balogun, who was frequently enraged and treated both staff and patients like ignorant children who were about to be severely punished. Behind her back, we called her Beretta Blowgun. I'd seen her argue bitterly with doctors in the hallway, telling them she was right, and they were wrong. Strictly verboten. Nurses may question doctors in private, civilly, not confront them.

One overcast morning, Carmen assigned me to sit with two female patients in Room 16. One woman required constant assistance for her stomach cancer, while the other, suffering from dementia, roamed the halls, prone to violence. Halfway through my shift, Beretta, who'd just come on duty as charge nurse, demanded to know why I sat in that room. I told her that was my assignment. She berated me for abandoning the nine patients for whom I would have been caring if I'd been working the floor. She ordered me to leave Room 16 and meet all those patients' needs by the end of my shift—what little was left of it.

When Beretta left the room, a kind-hearted RN named Sonya came in to provide meds to Ms. Clayton, the stomach cancer patient. Immediately afterward, Beretta, unaware of Sonya, returned and read me the riot act again for wasting a half-day. She again commanded me to fully meet the needs of my nine new patients before the end of the shift. When Beretta left, Sonya put a hand on my shoulder.

"Just ignore her," she said. "Beretta's crazy."

Freed from my room, shaking with anger, I complained about Beretta to Rose Oni. She asked Beretta to join us, so we each could tell our side of the story. Beretta denied everything. Rose allowed me to call Sonya as a witness. Although no one wanted to cross Beretta because she was so angry and vindictive, Sonya bravely confirmed my account. Clearly guilty, Beretta sobbed to avoid punishment.

I was so angry over my stressful day that I swam a mile at my local outdoor Olympic pool that afternoon; a mile swim usually has a great calming effect on me, but on this day I was still livid after my 72 laps. Upon arriving home, I had three drinks—I usually never consume alcohol after swimming because I already feel relaxed, and I virtually never have more than two drinks when I indulge. I complained bitterly to Elizabeth, and she became angry regarding how poorly I'd been treated. I didn't know it at the time but listening to these accounts eventually would become too painful for her to bear.

When I realized I was still furious at the way Beretta had treated me, I called in sick the next day. I didn't care whether Rose Oni figured out the correlation between the two events. I was sending a signal: when Beretta screams at me and there are no consequences for her, I decided, I'm going to be out ill the next day.

For months afterward, when I passed Beretta in the halls, I could tell she hated me and would do everything in her power to make me suffer. However, after management received years of complaints from nurses and CNAs about the mistreatment they received from Carmen and Beretta, an executive ordered them to cut it out immediately or face serious consequences. But I was too jaded to rejoice. Carmen and Berretta cleaned up their acts for only a few months before returning to their old ways with increased vigor.

Bad Nurses

So how were CNAs treated by the RNs? About half the time, the RNs were friendly and requested our help only when they really needed it. For example, some of our patients were quite large-bodied—the heaviest I'd seen was a woman weighing 1,000 pounds. Obviously, before a nurse repositioned an overweight patient, she phoned a floor CNA for help. In the case of the thousand-pound patient, four people moved her so we could clean her up after she soiled her bed. This operation required forty-five minutes. Good nurses don't mind feeding patients, changing their linens, bringing their patients ice water or wash-up supplies, and performing other hands-on tasks. Sometimes these nurses fell behind in their work or faced a chore that required two people, and they asked us to help them get caught up, which we were pleased to accommodate.

Then there were the lazy nurses who believed their sole mission was to dispense medications and chart patient information. During my first few years at Malmed, we had three such nurses. They phoned the floor CNAs every few minutes during the shift, asking us to perform all their hands-on duties. As a worst-case example, all three of these nurses would be working on the same day when there was only one floor CNA available. This meant the floor CNA tried her best to care for twenty-eight patients while also performing all the hands-on work for three nurses. Impossible, so inevitably one or more of the indolent nurses would get angry that a certain job didn't get performed, and, predictably, the most slothful RNs were also the quickest to complain to the charge nurse. A good charge nurse would shrug off the complaint because she knew the floor CNA was overloaded, but a bad charge nurse would seek out the assistant nurse and reprimand her, even if that person was in the break room.

Fuck You Chuck

Although our director, Victor Chukwu, was in charge of nursing on three units, he found plenty of time to annoy the hell out of his staff. For example, he prowled the break rooms on his floors, rummaging around in the refrigerators. If he found a lunch that didn't smell fresh, he pitched it into the trash. This left staff members frightened they'd take a break only to discover they had no food for the rest of their shift. This situation was especially worrisome for the RNs because they worked twelve-hour shifts at a hospital lacking a cafeteria.

Victor also enjoyed frequenting the break rooms and berating staff members. When the staff member in question became upset, Victor cracked a wide smile and said, "Just kidding." But that wasn't the end of it because Victor usually inserted a cruel kernel of truth into his insults, so he hurt his victims' feelings and humiliated them in front of their colleagues. No wonder the mean-spirited charge nurses didn't respect the sanctity of the break room. If this were a movie, an unhinged nurse demeaned by Victor would purposely collide with him in the hallway and inject him with a fatal dose of morphine.

Ill Treatment

So Malmed Memorial was not an ideal workplace, except for miraculous days of planetary alignment. This raises a final question. What was it like to be a patient there?

For the most part, our nurses took excellent care of their patients, most of whom were poor and fairly uneducated with the health problems attendant to this population. For example, we had many patients who were blind with amputated feet because they were diabetics who failed to follow the regimen recommended by their doctors; these patients are labeled "noncompliant," but these regimens often are onerous, prompting some healthcare professionals to say these patients are under a "burden of care" rather than noncompliant. We also had numerous heavy smokers with lung cancer and alcoholics who had destroyed their kidneys and livers.

However, just as there were nurses who mistreated the CNAs, there were also nurses who mistreated patients. For example, we had a patient who had lost the use of his legs. As a result, he spent most of his time on his back, and his bottom and lower back looked like bloody hamburger. These wounds needed to be covered at all times with a sterile dressing that should've been changed every other day. Our wound nurse discovered his dressing hadn't been changed in three and a half days.

Why? Because his slothful nurse, Pam Simpson, believed her sole duty was to dispense medication and chart. Like many of our nurses, Pam was only in nursing because of the high pay ($150,000 at our hospital; full-time RNs made $80/hour and worked 36 hours a week.), and she was so cold-hearted that many of her patients complained to me that she hated them.

I once answered the call light of a patient wailing with pain who asked me to please tell Pam she needed relief. She said I was the fifth person she'd asked. When I reported this patient's agony, Pam said, "Uh-huh," and kept on charting. I informed the charge nurse, Mary Savage, of the situation. When Pam still hadn't moved ten minutes later, Mary reproached her and forced her to medicate her patient.

Another nurse named Virginia Black gave a difficult patient she disliked a cold bed bath that left him screaming, even though hot water was readily available. She also approached an emaciated old man who lay sleeping with his back to her. His bottom was exposed through a gap in his hospital gown. Without a word, this nurse shoved him on his stomach and jammed a suppository up his rectum while he shrieked with pain and surprise. Why? Because, like Pam Simpson, she was only in nursing for the money, and she treated her patients as if they were pieces of meat. And I didn't report her because she was in the clique I've mentioned that extended into nursing management. Ironically, Virginia had a warm and outgoing personality regarding her fellow nurses, and she was quick to laugh and smile. One would never guess she treated her patients so poorly.

Finally, we admitted a mentally ill patient named Amy Sullivan to our floor because she'd swallowed a combination of razor blades and batteries, an act she'd performed many times before. Her assigned nurse, Carla Kilgore, one of our most phlegmatic and vicious ones, walked into her room for the first time and harangued her.

"Don't you have any common sense?" she said. "Why'd you do it—were you seeking attention? Don't you think that's a really stupid way to go about it?"

Poor Amy, who was obese and mentally ill, had hoped a compassionate and non-judgmental healthcare professional would provide a ray of sunshine to return her to good health, but she sobbed

48

because she realized she'd fallen into a black hole of cruelty.

Descent

Two months later, my wife, Elizabeth, and I left town for a much-needed weekend getaway. We desired a break from our stressful jobs, and our marriage had become strained, mainly because I couldn't stop talking about how mistreated I felt at work.

Elizabeth's nemesis at the veterinary hospital, where she worked as the head of the front office, was Amanda, a large-bodied, 6'4" head veterinary technician who frequently bullied and trash-talked my wife and her front-office compatriots. Elizabeth complained about her most days when she came home from work.

I didn't mind listening, even though I felt hurt, angry, and powerless when I heard about Elizabeth's tales of workplace mistreatment. My job was to listen and provide support. Also, in the long run, I figured Amanda would either shape up or ship out, since she was a highly visible misbehaving employee with a growing cadre of enemies. And, as it turned out, I was right. Soon after our trip, her supervisor discovered Amanda had been padding her hours for months, drawing pay for unworked time; she was fired.

However, when I told Elizabeth about my bad days at work, which consisted mainly of shouting and false accusations from Carmen Sanchez and Berretta Blowgun, she would cringe and silence me.

"I'm sorry," she said. "I can't listen to these stories anymore. They're too painful. And your job is dragging you down—you're distant, brooding, and depressed. You've lost your enthusiasm for life. If you need to talk to someone, talk to Ginger. And if you have to change jobs, do so. You can always come to me if you want to discuss a major decision you're considering."

She was right. Malmed Memorial was an evil, soul-consuming place. I promised Elizabeth I would toughen up, recover my former self, and protect her from the poison.

Speaking of poison, I'd recently come across a flyer in the breakroom listing key issues our union was fighting at Malmed: no more management disrespect and abuse, no more budget cuts to patient care, no more favoritism, and no more toxic work environment. It felt great to have a third party validate my issues with the hospital; however, I had no faith we'd see much in the way of improvement.

We chose the town of Murphys as our get-away destination, which was about a three-hour drive from our home. Nestled in the Sierra foothills, Murphys is an old gold rush town with a reputation as a great place to relax and have fun. One glance along Main Street confirmed this: an art gallery, a bookstore, a museum, the entrance to a cavern, and a plethora of wine tasting rooms and restaurants, which were full of seemingly happy and relaxed customers. The whole town exuded an aura of pleasure and ease, accented by the crisp mountain air. At first glance, the only amenity missing was a spa with hot tubs and massages, but I was certain there was one tucked away somewhere.

After casing Main Street, we discovered a quaint café in a shady courtyard set far back from the street, where our cheerful and attentive waitress served us delicious lunches. Sipping a chilled chardonnay with a wonderfully silky finish, we watched the play of light and shadow as the pleasant breeze jostled the multi-colored sun umbrellas above the tables. The bright sunshades reminded me of balloons at a carnival with their hypnotic swaying. We ate in companionable silence punctuated by small talk. I felt highly relaxed but alert and present, Elizabeth appearing to feel the same.

"There you are," she said, leaning across the table to kiss me.

"Missed you," I said. "Hey, you want to check out that cavern?"

"Love to," she said, her face brightening.

When we first met, I was crazed to hike, bike, and swim. Elizabeth was in pretty good shape, but she lost 25 pounds keeping pace with me. She was delighted I was active and lean and likely to keep her that way as well. However, after my two years of unemployment, I obtained several part-time jobs (swim team coach and instructor, winery tasting room host) that required me to work weekends. This caused our hiking and biking to fall by the wayside and remained when I joined Malmed Memorial and toiled weekends there as well. However, we'd recently coordinated our work schedules, so we had every other weekend off together, and Elizabeth expressed a strong interest in returning to our high level of physical activity. My suggestion that we explore the cave was just what she wanted to hear.

After lunch, we walked over to the cavern entrance. I'd recently had my right knee replaced, but I was walking pretty well, albeit slowly, and not in much pain, so I felt confident I could maneuver reasonably well in the cave.

Once we entered the storefront housing the mouth of the cavern and paid, we followed our tour guide down a long staircase of uneven and make-shift steps, descending into what appeared to be a deep cavity. Our guide called out that the staircase had 300 steps. I told Elizabeth to go ahead, and she and the other tourists quickly disappeared into the dim light ahead of me.

I made my way down slowly, carefully choosing my steps and thinking about the long climb I'd have to make back up. After a few minutes, I was the only person on the staircase, and I heard our guide begin his lecture, occasionally catching a glimpse of his flashlight beam illuminating the pink and yellow cavern walls, but mostly the only thing I could see was the faint steps ahead of me. I plodded on, continuing to hear our guide lecturing but not able to discern his words.

After what seemed like an eternity, I reached the cave floor, just in time to hear our tour guide say, "Thanks, that concludes our tour. Please head back up the steps and be sure to visit our gift shop."

Elizabeth looked at me with sympathetic humor. "Glad you could make it," she said. "Come on, I'll meet you back topside and buy you a drink!"

Childhood

I was no stranger to violence when I signed on with Malmed Memorial. When I was a small boy, Mrs. Cunningham, one of my mother's friends from church, visited our house with her young son, Webster, a red-headed hellion known for leaving a wide path of destruction in his wake. Before they arrived, my mother warned me my father would "blister my bottom" if I allowed Webster to damage any aspect of our home. He ran through our house brandishing a toy metal six-shooter. I became his shadow, following on his heels and keeping a keen eye out for any attempts on his part to wreak destruction.

However, I lowered my guard for a single minute, ducking into the bathroom for a quick pee. When I came out, I found my mother staring in horror at Webster's gun, which lay atop my father's prized mahogany stereo.

My mother's eyes filled with fury.

"I was going to the bathroom when it happened," I said. I gently lifted the pistol off the well-polished cabinet. "Look, there's no scratches."

My mother's expression didn't change.

After our company left, I desperately pleaded my case again, but my mother was livid.

"Just wait until your father gets home," she said.

I retreated in a terrified panic to my room, knowing exactly what was coming. I played quietly with my stuffed animals, but my fear never subsided. In fact, it continued to grow, causing tremendous sickening pain in my stomach. I wished I were dead. When it was time for my father to arrive, I changed into my pajamas and hid in the back of my bedroom closet. As soon as he came through the front door, my mother spoke to him, and he burst into my bedroom with a roar. He hauled me out of the closet, jerking my arm so hard I feared it would come out of its socket. Then the second part of the punishment ritual began. My father grabbed me by the back of the head and ground my forehead into his while he glared into my eyes with insane hatred. He growled.

As he dragged me to the bathroom, my mother said, "Take off his pajamas so it will hurt more."

My father clawed off my pajamas and struck my bottom a dozen hard blows with a thick homemade oak paddle while I screamed. The beating was unbelievably painful, and I was afraid he'd break my arm or fingers if I tried to shield my bottom. When my father finished, he shoved me back into my room and shut the door.

Despite my pain and tears, I was so angry I stuck out my tongue at the closed door. My father whipped open the door, saw my tongue out, and jerked me into the bathroom for a second beating just as brutal as the first.

The Redwood Screamer

Shortly after Elizabeth and I returned refreshed from our brief vacation in Murphys, I worked the floor, assisting fourteen patients and their RNs. Throughout my shift, I heard a patient with a booming voice screaming for help, but I never saw any nurses rushing toward his room. I wasn't responsible for that patient, but I wanted to make sure he was receiving proper care, so I asked his nurse, Janice, what was going on.

"He's a really unfortunate case," she said. "He's a ninety-one-year-old guy with pneumonia and dementia who fell and badly bruised the right side of his body. Even though he's on plenty of morphine and isn't in pain, he's fixated on the fact that he's hurt and needs help—we can't break through his dementia to convince him otherwise."

The next day, Carmen assigned me to care for this patient, Mr. Barrington. Mr. Barrington, or Barry as he was called, was at least six feet three and solid, reminding me of a giant sequoia. He wasn't fat, but he was dense and heavy, and it took several nurses to turn him in bed.

At first, his nearly deafening cries were unnerving, but I soon became accustomed to them.

"Help! Help!" he called out.

"I'm right here, Barry," I said. "How can I assist you?"

"My right side is killing me!"

"Your nurse gave you morphine an hour ago. You should feel pretty comfortable right now, but I'll ask her if there's anything else we can do for your pain."

"Help! Help!"

"Barry, what can I do for you?"

"I have to pee!"

I helped Barry pee into a hand-held plastic urinal. For male patients who were bed-ridden and incontinent, we often placed condom catheters over their penises so they could urinate into a collection bag hanging from their bed. I'd been briefed by the assistant nurse on the previous shift that Barry was incontinent, although he often asked for a urinal. I noticed Barry was not wearing a condom catheter, and I wondered why.

Upon examination, I learned Barry had a small, retracted penis inside a long foreskin. When I pushed back the foreskin, I saw his penis was badly broken out into a "diaper rash." I realized Barry's penis required frequent cleaning, followed by the application of a moisture barrier ointment to prevent urine from touching and burning his skin.

Just as I reached this conclusion, our wound care nurse, Ursula, came into the room to check on Barry.

"So you notice he's not a good candidate for a condom cath," she said. "I'm going to show you how to arrange some Ultrasorb pads so he can pee into them without wetting his skin or bed. You can change out the pads as needed."

Ursula demonstrated, and I understood it. Then she examined several wounds Barry had sustained in his fall and left the room.

"Help!" Barry shouted again.

"Yes, I'm right here," I said.

"My right side is killing me!" he said. "And I need to pee!"

I felt a moment's irritation. However, I thought about things from his point of view, and I soon felt deep empathy for him. Here was a confused old guy lying helpless and hurt in a hospital bed who thought he was in constant pain and was obsessed with urinating every few minutes. Also, he was a giant of a man, and I wondered if his morphine dosage was strong enough to truly make him comfortable.

On top of that, he had pneumonia and was in danger of suffocating in his phlegm. If we caught it building up in his throat, his nurse or I could perform a light suction; if the condition had come on suddenly, we had to notify Respiratory Therapy immediately so they could provide a deep suction. Barry's only moments of peace were the blessed times he drifted off to sleep.

Barry's pureed breakfast arrived, and I fed him tiny bites of eggs and potatoes because he was on aspiration precaution, which meant he had swallowing issues and ran the risk of inhaling food into his lungs. In elderly people like Barry, the signal from the brain telling the throat to swallow can be weakened. This was the case with Barry, but his condition was more complex because the contours of his throat had been altered by a previous surgery, perhaps for throat cancer.

While I fed Barry, my thoughts wandered to my father, also a ninety-one-year-old victim of dementia, who lay in his bed in a memory care unit in my boyhood town of Arlington, Virginia, where he faced the same swallowing difficulty as Barry. I felt as if I were simultaneously trying to help Barry and my father swallow successfully.

My feelings toward my father were complex. I felt basic human sympathy regarding his plight; otherwise, I was indifferent. The out-of-control spankings ended when I was twelve turning thirteen, and my conscious fury toward him had dissipated. Still, I had nightmares in which I screamed at him and tried to stab, strangle, or shoot him. Unlike my brother, Danny, who as an adult, could crack our father up with a spontaneous joke or fascinate him with the details of how a certain object was constructed, maintained, or repaired, I held myself at a cautious emotional distance from him, and he never tried to get to know me.

Also, he mistreated us beyond out-of-control spankings and into the realm of deep, pre-meditated cruelty. Once during our childhood, Danny hung out with our father in his basement workshop.

Our father honed an ax until it was razor-sharp; then he handed it to Danny and said, "Test this blade for me." When Danny tapped the blade against his palm; blood blossomed into a long cut.

My father was dying, and I frequently thought about how I'd feel when that happened. I correctly speculated I'd experience a mix of indifference and sadness that we'd never been close. Also, to be honest, I'd feel relief his suffering (advanced dementia and several strokes) was over, and the monster who'd terrorized my childhood—and led me to publish my previous memoir, *Less than Human*—was finally dead.

*****

Despite a few touch-and-go moments, Barry ate his entire breakfast. When he finished, I cleaned out his mouth with a soft sponge on a stick I'd soaked in a 50/50 mixture of water and mouthwash.

Shortly afterward, Barry's wife, Ethel, and his home caregiver, Reese, arrived to sit with him for a half-day. I liked Ethel immediately. She had silver hair, a kind face with laugh lines, and a sharp mind. She immediately thanked me for caring for Barry. Reese, a husky redhead, checked on Barry, but soon warmed up to me when she learned he'd eaten his entire breakfast, I'd provided oral care, and I was doing everything I could to treat the rash on his penis and keep his throat clear.

Reese's presence was a bit unusual. She was on the clock, paid by Ethel to care for Barry as well as supervise his nursing care and point out any deficiencies. Over the days Barry was with us, many of the nurses and assistant nurses developed a strong dislike for Reese because she was an outsider telling them how to do their jobs. This usually would be a sore point with me as well, but I found Reese's occasional suggestions reasonable, and they didn't bother me.

"This situation is just so sad," Ethel said. "A year ago, Barry was completely healthy, and we visited several European cities and had a wonderful time. He practically bounded up the steps at the Eiffel Tower, and he wanted to run with the bulls in Pamplona, until I put my foot down. He's always been this giant, active guy who could do whatever he wanted. This last year has been so hard for him."

Barry's personality was almost entirely submerged beneath his suffering, but I caught glimpses of it now and then. One day, before Ethel arrived, I told Barry she was coming to visit, and I mentioned I liked her.

He surprised me by saying, "Yeah, I like her, too!"

My charge nurses seemed to recognize I was successful at both caring for Barry and getting along with Ethel and especially Reese. They often assigned me to care for him, but not always. On other days, a patient care technician named Zoe sat with him.

Here's the difference between an assistant nurse and a patient care technician at our hospital. An assistant nurse has medical training and a Certified Nursing Assistant license from the California Department of Public Health. For example, I have six months of medical training and a CNA license as well as a certificate qualifying me to work in an acute care environment, such as a hospital. In addition, assistant nurses have to take and pass forty-eight hours of continuing education nursing classes every two years to maintain their licenses.

By contrast, patient care technicians don't have any licenses or nurse training. They typically are young people who just sit with patients and summon nurses if anything seems wrong. The patient care technician position was created by our unpopular nursing director, Victor Chukwu, who constantly slashed our budget, often endangering patients and staff with his reckless decisions. Our union suspected Victor was planning to replace CNAs with patient care technicians, but they headed him off at the pass by incorporating new language into our contract.

Ethel and Reese constantly scolded Zoe and complained to Carmen about her failure to properly feed him, provide oral care, suction the phlegm out of his throat, and keep his diaper rash under control.

The two women were furious at the situation, yet the charge nurses continued to assign Zoe to sit with Barry on numerous occasions. On her first day with Barry, I showed Zoe how to arrange the Ultrasorb pads to minimize him getting urine on his skin and bed. When I entered his room briefly later on, I noticed she'd used thin blue pads with almost no absorbency; they might be okay to put under the leg of someone with a slightly oozing wound, but they weren't designed to soak up urine.

I continued to care for Barry periodically. Our speech therapist frequently tested his swallowing ability, which plummeted. Soon, nobody, including Reese and me, could get Barry to swallow anything. His brain had stopped broadcasting the signal telling his throat to swallow. His doctor broke this news to Ethel and Reese and didn't recommend that a feeding (PEG) tube be surgically inserted in his stomach.

"I'm sorry I don't have better news," said Dr. Hanson. "I think the best thing is for you to bring Barry home, keep him as comfortable as possible, and engage hospice care."

Ethel and Reese thanked the doctor without argument. They'd been with Barry four hours a day for several weeks, and they'd come to accept his condition. I was glad Dr. Hanson broke the news. She was compassionate and clear in her explanations, and she treated me as a high-quality caregiver, always saying hello.

Barry left the hospital on an ambulance gurney, accompanied by Ethel and Reese. I never saw them again. A week later, my father died, having lost the ability to swallow.

Learning to Fly

Carmen assigned me to sit with a fifty-nine-year-old male patient on a psychiatric 5150 hold because he was bipolar, homicidal, and suicidal. When I entered his room, a shirtless Tom Petty lookalike with a large dressing covering a stab wound in his chest regarded me from his bed.

"Howdy!" he said. "Randy Richmond at your service!"

He laughed at my expression. "This is going to be great," he said. "I can tell you're a rock 'n' roller 'cause you think I look like Tom Petty, am I right?"

"You nailed it," I said.

"Hey, I've got this sweet little radio here. Tell me what you think." He cranked the volume and Led Zeppelin's "Black Dog" blasted forth. He waggled his eyebrows.

"Great tunes," I said.

"Fucking-A," he said. "Let's rock!"

I love classic rock, so I enjoyed the music with Randy while I charted some basic information about his current status into the computer.

After a while, Randy became bored with the radio and tuned his TV to the Discovery Channel, which he watched in fascination for hours. At first, we took in several episodes of *Fast N' Loud*, in which Richard Rawlings and his Gas Monkey Garage compatriots buy beat-up classic cars, renovate them, and attempt to sell them for a profit. Randy knew his classic cars and gave me a running commentary about the automobiles on the show.

"Oh my God," he said. "That Shelby's worth way more than that!"

I made a note to mention cars as a topic if Randy and I ran out of things to say. I'm not an auto aficionado, but I knew all I had to do was bring up the subject and Randy would hold forth.

However, I discovered Randy's true passion as we watched Mike Kennedy on *Airplane Repo* repossess a jet. At the end of the episode, Randy muted the TV.

"Allen, I'll tell you," he said. "If I could only have two things in this world, it would be a pilot's license and a Cessna 172 Skyhawk. Just thinking about flying through the wild blue yonder brings peace and joy to my heart."

"I hope you can achieve that dream," I said.

"I'm working on it, man, but life's been hard. I'm homeless. My parents are dead from alcohol and drugs, and all of my friends are dead or in jail. And I'm fucking bipolar. And I want to hurt people real bad, which makes me a monster, and then I feel like killing myself. I use hard drugs to live with myself, but they don't help. The one thing I had going for me was that I was taking online classes to get my bachelor's degree, until someone stabbed me and stole my laptop."

Just then, Randy's nurse, Janice, knocked on the door and entered. I liked her—she was a skilled RN with a great bedside manner.

"Good morning, Mr. Richmond," she said, smiling. "I've got several medications for you, and I'll explain what each one's for."

Randy flew into a rage. "You're not explaining shit to me, you stupid bitch. Can't you see I'm talking to my friend, Allen? Get the fuck out of my room!" he shouted.

Janice beat a hasty retreat, closing the door a split second before Randy hurled his pitcher of ice water against it.

Randy sat with his head bowed for a silent minute; then he said, "Sorry man, I know that wasn't cool. It's just that the doctors and nurses here drive me ape-shit. They all look down their noses at me because they think I'm a bipolar junkie who's never going to amount to anything."

"Then show them they're wrong," I said. "You've got great potential. Do whatever you need to stay clear-minded and straight, get your college degree, and become a pilot."

"Man, there's something about you," Randy said. "I've wanted to hurt every doctor, nurse, and sitter, but you're different—you have a calming influence on me. I feel normal when it's just you and me."

I cleaned up the spilled water, and the rest of my shift passed without incident, except Randy shouted his doctor out of the room when she looked in on him.

Driving home that evening, I thought about stopping by Barnes & Noble to pick up some small-craft aviation magazines for him, but traffic was snarled, and the store was a significant distance out of my way.

The next morning in our nurses' huddle, I learned I'd been assigned to sit with Randy again. After the meeting, Carmen took me aside and said, "Allen, you're absolutely not allowed to leave the patient's room. Mr. Richmond tried to hang himself last night. Please be careful."

When I entered Randy's room, his head was bowed, and he had a glum expression, but he brightened when he saw me.

"Man, am I glad to see you!" he said.

"Good to see you," I said. "What happened last night?"

Randy grinned. "Well, last night my sitter was this big fat, mean, ugly bitch, and I was trying to think how to fuck her over. And I hate being here, and I hate wanting to hurt people, so I was also thinking about how to off myself. Then I came up with this brilliant plan. I told the bitch I was really thirsty, and I sent her to get a bunch of orange juices and a bucket of ice. As soon as she was gone, I tied my bedsheet to the hook on the back of the bathroom door, ran the sheet over the top, and tried to hang myself from the front of the door. I dropped with my knees bent, but I didn't snap my neck. Then I was just slowly strangling there when the bitch came back, screamed, and saved my life."

"Well," I said. "I'm glad you're still here. How's your throat?"

"A little sore, not too bad."

I sat with Randy for a week. He was always delighted to see me and sad when I left. We talked rock and roll and TV shows from the sixties and seventies, and we watched the Discovery Channel. There was a close feeling between us, like we were friends or brothers. Although he still screamed at doctors, nurses, and social workers who entered his room, he never had a cross word for me, and he seemed content and frequently mentioned how he was going to stick to the plan we'd made for him.

Here was a bright guy with a mostly pleasant personality who'd had the misfortune to be born into mental illness, poverty, and drug addiction. If he'd stick to his meds, lay off heroin and cocaine, and get his college degree, he just might fulfill his dreams or at least find a modicum of happiness or contentment.

At the end of the week, Randy's doctor came to visit him several times, and he was cordial and polite toward her. He'd also been taking his psych meds without a fuss for the last few days.

"Randy, I'm so proud of you," said Dr. Cantrell. She explained she was transferring him to a psychiatric hospital from which she expected him to be quickly discharged.

Randy smiled and stuck out his hand. After a moment of hesitation, Dr. Cantrell put her hand in his, and Randy gently shook it.

On the day Randy's ambulance ride was due at 4:00 p.m., we sat in our unit's sunny lounge a little before 3:30 p.m., my quitting time.

"Shit, Allen, I'm going to miss you," he said.

"Same here," I said. I knew Randy faced steep odds in overcoming mental illness and drug addiction, but I had high hopes for him.

"Would you mind giving me your contact information?" he asked. "I'd really like to stay in touch."

I nodded, thinking hard about whether I wanted to share my coordinates. On one hand, maybe I could be part of Randy's support system as he improved his life. On the other, his mental illness and ferocity might ruin mine.

Randy looked at me, having momentarily forgotten his request. "You know," he said. "I used to have a good time living with my buddies on the streets of San Francisco. I can tell you this now because they're all dead. We all had these long knives for self-defense, but we'd also get high and stab people for fun. There's a trick to it. You can hold a finger on each side of the blade with one hand and strike with the other, so the blade only goes in as deep as your fingers, not all the way to the hilt. So you can nail someone without making it fatal. It's really fun."

I smiled with my best poker face. When the ambulance crew and a Care Management staffer approached a moment later with paper-work for Randy to complete, I slipped away, punched out, and fled home.

Flight Three: 2016

Hallway of a Thousand Screams

Disarmament

At the end of an uneventful week, I sat in a two-patient room. One, an elderly man with dementia, was a high fall risk, while the other, a psychotic named Phil Grierson, would wake up famished and pace his room while screaming for his breakfast. Phil was skeletal with long, greasy hair, despite his bald spot. He'd been diagnosed as a psychotic heroin addict. This didn't surprise me—many mentally ill patients self-medicate with alcohol and drugs, the three most popular being heroin, cocaine, and meth.

I ordered Phil's breakfast for him at 7:30 a.m. I didn't want to tell the kitchen within Phil's hearing to provide plastic utensils because Phil was psychotic. My rule was don't anger psychotic patients with foul tempers. The breakfast was supposed to arrive by 8:30, but despite multiple calls to the kitchen, the food didn't appear until 10:30. While I was caring for the elderly gentleman, the tray passer walked into the room and set the meal down in front of a by-then-hunger-crazed Phil, who sat on the edge of his bed.

As bad luck would have it, Carmen walked by the room at that precise moment, spied the metal silverware, and ordered me to take it away. I went to the door to explain the dangerous situation.

"Remove the silverware!" she demanded.

I managed to confiscate the silverware, but Phil flew into a rage. Carmen brought him a plastic fork and spoon. Phil was so hungry he used these to shovel food into his mouth, but when he finished eating, he shouted at Carmen and me for not allowing him to have metal silverware or a knife of any kind. Finally, he settled down and decided to take a shower. When I cracked open the door to the bathroom and explained I was required to keep it open for safety, he slammed it.

At Malmed Memorial, no one seemed to care about the CNAs' safety, except for the CNAs. The utensil policy was a case in point. Doctors and RNs were supposed to order the kitchen not to provide silverware to combative and mentally ill patients, but they rarely followed this guideline. It was difficult for CNAs to intercept and replace the silverware before it fell into the patient's hands, and confiscating it was perilous.

Also, calling for help if we were attacked was virtually impossible. The combative and suicidal patients' phones were often removed from their rooms because these patients might have tried to hang or strangle themselves with the long cords or call 911 and report they were being held prisoner. The hospital had an internal phone network, but sitters were not provided with the blue cell phones with access to this network.

The hospital had many other policies that placed staff and patients in harm's way. For example, the hospital was debt-burdened, so the entire facility was on a shoe-string budget. This meant old and busted-up computers, medication scanners, and vital sign machines. I once heard a patient cry out for God to kill him because he couldn't bear his back pain any longer. His desperate and frustrated nurse went through seven medication scanners before he found one that worked so he could relieve his patient's pain.

As another example, our doctors were mysteriously reluctant to sedate or restrain combative psych patients. I understand why doctors didn't want to prescribe sedatives for patients recovering from brain injuries—obviously, the brain needs to function at full-throttle while healing. Still, there were many patients at Malmed Memorial who were mentally ill and hostile, while lacking head injuries, low blood pressure, and other contraindications that would prevent a doctor from sedating them. I don't understand why these patients were not sedated when they posed a threat to themselves or others, but I couldn't ask, since assistant nurses weren't allowed to talk with doctors unless they asked us questions about their patients, or we had vital information to convey.

At this point, the rest of the problems on our unit could be attributed to Victor and his policies. While he reigned as our director, he slashed his meager budget in a manner that greatly increased danger to patients and staff while making him look like a hero to his superiors and supposedly ensuring job security.

I'm pleased to announce Victor's use of four-patient sitter rooms eventually came back to bite him. An emergency room doctor entered one of these rooms to follow up with a trauma patient who'd been stabilized and transferred to our unit. She was so appalled by the conditions there, which included an extremely overloaded assistant nurse and several difficult-to-control psychiatric patients, she reported Fuck You Chuck to the California Department of Public Health and the hospital's executives. Victor immediately eliminated four-patient hell-hole rooms. We rejoiced, although it was frustrating Victor never got fired for his colossal screw-ups back then.

An employee satisfaction survey taken around this time determined Malmed Memorial's nurses felt highly frustrated regarding their ability to provide high-quality patient care. Consequently, our manager, Rose Oni, rounded up the nurses on our unit and asked them why they were so discontented. I saw the whiteboard after their session. The first three items on their list of barriers to outstanding care were: broken equipment, short staffing, and four-patient sitter rooms.

The day after I sat with Phil Grierson, I wrote a brief email to my boss, Rose, urging her to reinforce the policy requiring all aggressive and suicidal patients to receive plastic utensils from the kitchen. I also asked her to please buy a few more blue hospital cell phones so CNAs could access them while sitting. That was years ago, and I never received a reply.

Alligator

When my brother, Danny, and I were in elementary school, we visited our grandfather and his second wife in Florida, where they owned a house on a lake. This body of water teemed with wildlife, including large iridescent dragonflies and an adult alligator that occasionally sunned itself in our grandparents' backyard.

As soon as we arrived and carried in the luggage, my father said, "Boys, we want some adult time—go outside and play."

"But it's really hot and humid," I protested. "We'll roast out there, unless it's okay to swim?"

I thought about how refreshing a dip in the lake might feel, but I was afraid of the alligator.

"Swimming's fine," my mother said. "Hurry up and unpack your bathing suits, and don't track any water or sand back into the house."

"But what about the alligator?" I said.

"Stop whining and do as your mother says," my father said.

With fishing gear loaned to us by our grandfather, Danny and I positioned ourselves on an old, warped pier and cast our spinners out into the murky water. After a couple of sweltering hours without any bites, I decided to swim. Danny refused to budge, his eyes scanning the russet surface for the alligator.

I stepped into the lake, thick mud oozing between my toes and spiky plants pin-pricking my soles. I waded into the pleasantly cool but swampy-smelling water until I was up to my waist. Then I carefully surveyed the lake. The day was scorching, I wanted to plunge into the water and swim, but a deeper instinct reminded me that at any moment I could be prey. I froze. Part of me felt safe because our parents knew I was swimming, but I was also afraid I'd get snapped up into the alligator's jaws.

Although I kept my eyes peeled for any creatures near me, a turtle suddenly popped its head out of the water a foot away, scaring the bejesus out of me.

Monty Python Revisited

One day, I walked past the room of a one-legged patient named Mr. Stanley. Although he had a burning desire to flee the hospital, none of the charge nurses took this threat seriously, and none assigned a CNA to sit with him. When I glanced into his room, he was on the floor, slithering on his stomach toward the door.

"Mr. Stanley," I said. "What're you doing? Did you fall? Are you okay?"

"I'm getting the fuck out of here!" he shouted. "Get out of my way, or I'll bite the shit out of your ankles!"

Cliffhanger without Resolution

Sometimes when CNAs cared for a patient, we got wrapped up in an intriguing story surrounding his or her admission, but we didn't necessarily learn how the tale ended. For example, I sat with a psychotic twenty-year-old man who'd jumped out a fourth-story window; he landed upright, breaking both feet and ankles. His name was George Day, and he thrashed wildly in his bed, talking to himself, crying out, and moaning, even in his sleep. His nurse, working closely with his doctor, gave him an increasing amount of painkillers and sedatives until he finally lay still and slept peacefully for hours.

Toward the end of George's long nap, his mother visited his room. She introduced herself as Mary. She was attractive and elegantly dressed in black and gray, with raven hair cut stylishly short. She looked like a highly competent executive secretary, which helped me believe her incredible story.

"George is an addict," she said. "But he's been doing really well. I found him this great drug-free group home, where he's been living and staying clean for the last two years. He's been going to college. But his father, Tom—my ex-husband—recently convinced George to come live with a friend of Tom's named Charlie. He bought George a gigantic TV as a bribe. So George went, and he relapsed. He does meth, and it makes him psychotic.

"As far as I've been able to piece together what happened last night, George was at his father's, high on meth and psychotic. Tom was afraid of him and sprayed him in the face with mace. George jumped out of the window to get away from the mace. A neighbor who watches out for George and has my phone number called me. When I got there, George was writhing on the ground with broken feet and ankles while Tom and Charlie just stood looking at him as if nothing were wrong."

At this point, George woke up, clear-headed now. "That's not the whole story, Mom," he said. "When I was on the ground, Charlie held a knife to my throat. I thought he was going to kill me." He touched a red area near his Adam's apple. "Check this out—this is where the knife started to cut me."

We inspected the spot; George sported a thin red line that definitely could have been made by a knife.

Mary's brown eyes were large and teary. She was terrified Tom might attempt to kill George. She told me Tom had molested George as a boy, and George had been working on this issue in therapy and talking about it recently. Ironically, Mary told me, Tom was a doctor who directed a prestigious drug rehab center. If the sexual abuse stories became widespread, they could destroy his reputation and livelihood.

Just then, George's room phone rang.

"Please answer it," he said, nodding at me.

"Hello," I said. "Who's calling, please?"

"I'm trying to reach George Day. This is his father."

"Just a second, sir," I said, holding my hand over the mouthpiece. "It's his father," I whispered.

George and his mother vigorously shook their heads.

"I don't want to talk to him," George said.

"Please get him off the line," said Mary.

"I'm sorry, sir," I said. "But he's asleep, and I've got orders not to wake him. Feel free to try again later. Thanks." I hung up.

Mary wrung her hands. She told me Tom had located George because he was a doctor who could find out anything he wanted— she hadn't told him the ambulance's destination. She said he was a sociopath who was skilled at fooling people, and she was afraid he'd secretly inject George with something fatal to keep his mouth shut. She begged me to alert his nurse and social worker about the situation, so he could change rooms and be listed under a fake name.

I ran and spoke to George's nurse, Penny, who sat at the station just outside his room. I explained the situation; she immediately picked up the receiver, dialing a social worker.

When I returned to George's room, Mary thanked me profusely and told me she would work to transfer George to Kaiser, where he was a member.

I glanced at the clock. 3:30 p.m. Time to punch out. I said goodbye to George and Mary.

In general, I believed their story, partly because my own history is hard for some people to fathom, but Mary's tale was so far-fetched I had what Alfred Hitchcock might have called a shadow of a doubt. I wanted to learn more. But when I returned to the hospital the next day, George had vanished, presumably transferred to Kaiser, and there weren't any nurses on duty who knew what had happened to him.

No Good Deed Goes Unpunished

After our morning huddle that same day, I sat with an elderly gentleman with dementia who could barely walk. My primary job was to prevent him from getting out of bed and falling. When 11:00 a.m. rolled around, the patient's nurse, Penny, that foul-tempered woman with no compassion who was only in nursing for the high pay, relieved me so I could take eight vital signs.

I quickly took the vital signs in Rooms 1 and 2. However, when I entered Room 3, an emergency was in progress. The patient, Ms. Wong, an elderly woman I liked, was vomiting while her nurse, Tammy, held a basin for her and a volunteer named Steve stood by to offer any assistance.

"Allen, quick, please get orthostatic vital signs," Tammy said. "Ms. Wong is very ill, and her doctor's waiting for the results."

Orthostatic vital signs are taken while the patient is lying down, then sitting, then standing. In the past, I've taken orthostatic vital signs to help doctors diagnose orthostatic hypotension (sudden low blood pressure when a patient sits or stands). However, since I entered Ms. Wong's room in mid-emergency, I don't know exactly why her doctor ordered the procedure. Sometimes CNAs don't know the endings of patients' stories. In other cases, like this one, we encounter a patient in the middle of their story and don't fully understand its beginning or context.

I took Ms. Wong's temperature with a forehead scanner, her pulse, blood pressure, respirations, and blood oxygen saturation level. Normal blood pressure is around 120/80, but Ms. Wong's was dangerously high at 205/106.

"My head's killing me," said Ms. Wong before vomiting again.

Tammy's phone rang. "Yes, doctor," she said. "We're taking them now. Supine blood pressure is 205 over 106. Yes, we'll take the rest right away."

"Okay," Tammy said. "We need to sit her up now, but we have to be really gentle because Ms. Wong has an injured back. We have to go slow and easy."

The three of us carefully eased her into a sitting position. Between bouts of vomiting, Ms. Wong screamed with back pain. I took her sitting vital signs, and then, with even more vomiting and screaming on her part, we helped Ms. Wong get shakily to her feet.

As soon as I collected Ms. Wong's standing vital signs, Tammy said, "Allen, quick, run to a computer and chart the orthostatic vital signs. Do you know how?"

"Yes," I said as I bolted for the nearest nurses' station. I logged into a computer and began charting.

Just then, Penny stuck her head out of the door of the room where she was relieving me. When she saw me charting at the nurses' station, she became enraged.

"Allen, what the hell are you doing?" she demanded.

"I'm charting emergency data for a doctor," I said. "I'll talk to you in a second when I'm finished."

"I'm not listening to your bullshit excuses!" she said. "You've had me trapped in that room, and I have patients to medicate!" She abandoned the patient, entered a medication prep room, and slammed the door.

So, within a few seconds, I went from feeling proud I'd shown grace under pressure and possibly helped save a patient's life to once again feeling trembling anger and anxiety from working at a hospital where nurses threw temper tantrums and treated patients and CNAs like human refuse.

The year was 2016, and I'd been at Malmed Memorial for three years. By then, I despised the nurses and patients who victimized the CNAs. Now and then, I took days off, sometimes without pay, in an urgent attempt to relax and refresh. Worse, I found it hard to process such harsh treatment, so I brooded on it and talked about it incessantly with Elizabeth, which ruined many dinners and dates.

That night, I told Elizabeth the story of how three of us had helped a doctor take orthostatic vital signs during an emergency. I should have stopped there, but I went on to describe how much I detested Penny and all of the nurses and patients who mistreated CNAs. I knew I sounded like a broken record, but I couldn't shut up.

Elizabeth held up her hand. "Stop," she said. "I've told you; I can't listen to these stories anymore. I feel your pain, but I can't do anything about it. Either buck up and just tell me about your most interesting cases or get the hell out of that terrible place. I can't take this negative Debbie Downer crap every night at the dinner table."

Eyes are Always Watching

Our manager, Rose, had an administrative assistant named Donna who was in charge of scheduling work hours, vacations, and the like. While Rose always projected a calm and sweet demeanor, Donna was one of the most vicious staffers in our unit; she was universally despised by us CNAs. One of my colleagues called her "The Troll." She loved catching CNAs supposedly making mistakes, yelling at them, and then reporting these "mistakes" to Rose.

I once naively told Rose that Donna was strongly disliked by the CNAs. She simply nodded to acknowledge the information. I found out later Donna and Beretta Blowgun, our unit's nastiest employees, were close friends with Rose, and some staff members, including me, were convinced she used them to perform her dirty work so she could keep her image clean.

Rose had a rule that no two CNAs could eat morning snacks or lunches in the break room at the same time. But sometimes this happened because two nurses might simultaneously each ask a CNA to take a break. Thus, Alicia and I once found ourselves taking our morning breaks together. Donna burst into the break room, chewed us out, and immediately reported our unintentional transgression to Rose.

When I explained what had happened to Carmen, usually a stickler about the rules, she surprised me by saying in a lowered voice, "Listen, it doesn't bother me if two CNAs take a break at the same time—it's not the end of the world. But Rose insists on that rule, and you have to remember that eyes are always watching."

Death by Dentures

One morning when I was working on the floor, a nurse named Anna asked me to please help the patient in Room 17 put in his dentures.

"Mr. Woo's in a coma," she said. "But the family wants him to look nice."

Mr. Woo was a desiccated elderly man hooked up to a pulse-ox monitor that displayed his blood oxygen saturation level and heart rate. He looked peaceful, and I hated to disturb him. When I opened up his denture container, they reeked of bacteria and rotten food; I wouldn't have been surprised to see maggots swarming over the false teeth.

I spent the next half-hour cleaning the daylights out of the upper and lower dentures, completing the job by soaking them in mouthwash. When they were finally clean and odor-free, I approached Mr. Woo. The gentleman appeared to be in a peaceful, painless sleep. I noted a small red butterfly hanging from the door to his room—a signal to staff that a patient is dying and does not wish to be resuscitated. Again, I regretted having to disturb him. However, outraged family members made for one of the ugliest scenes in our hospital, so I decided to proceed, promising myself I'd stop if the process seemed too rough.

I gently opened Mr. Woo's mouth as wide as I could and tried to wiggle his upper denture into place. I kept listening and feeling for it to snap into place, but it wouldn't oblige. Suddenly, Mr. Woo's blood oxygen saturation level dropped to 0%, and his heart stopped beating. I quickly hooked him up to a vital sign machine, which detected faint vital signs and then none.

I was overwhelmed by guilt and regret. Even though I'd been gentle and acting under orders, I'd inadvertently killed Mr. Woo.

I immediately contacted his nurse, fearing severe criticism, but when Anna arrived, she glanced at him, grunted, and said, "Yeah, he's gone. I'll call his doctor."

Before exiting, she glanced back at me. "Hey," she said. "Don't worry. It was his time—you didn't do anything wrong."

Death Mask

A few days after my disastrous encounter with Mr. Woo, I entered the room of a middle-aged African American patient named Rodney Stacks to take his vital signs. Surrounded by his family, he was wearing a steamy BIPAP mask forcing oxygen into his lungs. I couldn't get a clear look at his face, but he appeared to be asleep and breathing heavily. When I attached the blood pressure cuff, his skin was warm, and his arm was easy to position.

The vital sign machine didn't detect any readings. This surprised me a little bit, but our Dinamaps were hard-used, and it wasn't uncommon for half of them to be broken.

"Don't worry," I told the family. "I don't think my machine's working—I'll get another one."

As I left the room, I realized it was possible the patient had died within the last few minutes; the forced air from the BIPAP could have created the illusion the patient was still breathing. I approached a long-experienced and nurturing charge nurse nicknamed Mama whom I liked and trusted. I told her what had just happened because the family might rush to her, and she knew every patient on the unit who desired emergency resuscitation.

Three hysterical sisters burst out of Room 21, surrounding us.

"Our father's dead, isn't he?" one of them asked.

"Why won't you tell us what's going on?" said another.

Mama raised her hand. "I'm going to examine your father right away, and Allen's going to get another vital sign machine," she said.

I grabbed another machine from the storage room. When I arrived back at Room 21, Mama had removed the patient's BIPAP mask and was checking for a pulse. I quickly connected the vital sign machine and again failed to get any readings.

Then Rodney's wife and daughters shouted, "Is he dead? Is he dead?"

Mama said, "I'm sorry. It looks like he's passed, but I'm not allowed to make that call. I'll have his doctor come immediately."

The women wept.

I wondered if the fact that they'd missed the exact moment of their loved one's passing intensified their grief.

Death Watch

One day, I sat with Mr. Jackson, a patient with severe COPD as well as kidney failure and bladder cancer that had metastasized. Despite several serious illnesses, he was usually chipper and feisty, as one of his doctors described him, but today he sat straight up in bed, unable to stay awake and breathe without great effort. Most people draw in 16 to 20 breaths per minute, but Mr. Jackson was only inhaling four times during that period.

Mr. Jackson was a sixty-two-year-old African American who'd lived a hard life, including serving time in prison. As I sat with him, presumably on death watch, several thoughts buzzed in my mind. First, I thought about how I'd helped Mr. Jackson take a shower just a couple of days earlier. He'd had a lot of energy, considering his ailments—too much, in fact. When I removed his gown before he stepped into the shower, I noticed he had a kidney drain coming out of each side of his lower back. This made sense—since his kidneys had shut down, these suction bulbs collected all the urine that normally would have been processed there. One drain hung loosely at his left side, but the other was stuck deep in the pocket of the gown we'd just removed.

"Mr. Jackson," I said. "Stop! Don't move until I get this kidney drain loose from your gown. I don't want you to pull it out."

But Mr. Jackson was looking forward to his shower, and he

climbed into it without pausing. Just as I'd feared, the end of the drainage tube surgically attached to his kidney jerked out of his back, followed by a trickle of blood. As soon as I had Mr. Jackson showered and safely back in bed, I notified his nurse, Helen Adebayo, who immediately contacted his doctor.

Now, as Helen, a rapid response nurse named Janelle, and his physician, Dr. Abassi, hovered over Mr. Jackson and discussed his condition, Dr. Abassi said, "He further damaged his kidneys when he pulled out that drain."

I felt a surge of guilt, but I also believed I'd done my best to protect Mr. Jackson from dislodging the urine collection bulb. I'd been using both hands to remove the apparatus, which was caught up in his gown pocket, and I'd commanded him to stop walking. With 20:20 hindsight, maybe I should have grabbed him and then worked on freeing the device, but I'd expected him to stop when I asked. He usually followed my instructions.

Then another thought struck me, not for the first time. I was a healthy, white male who swam a mile a day after work without much effort. However, I'd noticed many of my inner-city African American patients were extremely ill or dying by the time they reached my age—I was fifty-nine when caring for Mr. Jackson—an observation that saddened me.

My third thought was about the expressions of the two nurses and doctor in the room. Maybe Mr. Jackson hadn't been a model citizen, but everyone's face was strained with compassion and concern. Dying can be a hard business, and it was difficult for us to observe Mr. Jackson struggling for breath and consciousness. All that mattered was that he was a fellow human being whom we hated to see suffer.

At one point, everyone left the room, and I resumed my solo death watch. Right before she exited, Dr. Abassi said, "Mr. Jackson has COPD, so normal oxygen saturation for him is 85% to 92%. If he falls below 85%, please give him one liter of oxygen only—too much oxygen is bad for COPD patients."

Shortly afterward, Hannah, our unit's notoriously lazy CNA, relieved me so I could attend to one of the ten other patients I'd been assigned, despite my being on death watch with Mr. Jackson. I carefully explained the doctor's oxygen instructions. Hannah nodded, but I could tell she wasn't really listening, intent as she was on sitting down and goofing around on her cell phone, which, of course, was strictly forbidden.

"Are you sure you understand about the oxygen?" I said.

"Yes," she said. "Go take care of your other patients."

When I returned, Helen, Janelle, and Dr. Abassi were once again attending to Mr. Jackson, and two doctors stood just outside in the hall talking excitedly. Hannah left as soon as I entered the room.

"What happened?" I asked.

"Those doctors glanced in and thought Mr. Jackson was dead," Dr. Abassi said.

I noticed Hannah had disobeyed my instructions and put Mr. Jackson on two liters of oxygen. Almost all patients requiring oxygen at Malmed received two liters per minute.

"He's on two liters of oxygen," I said. "I left instructions for one liter if he desats below 85%. Want me to change it to one liter?"

"No, leave it for now," said Dr. Abassi. "I'm getting an idea. Mr. Jackson looks suspiciously like someone overdosing on opioids. Let's see what they gave him for pain last night." She consulted the bedside computer. "Yes, look," she said. "He received a strong dose of Dilaudid!"

She tapped rapidly on the keyboard, then turned to Helen. "I just ordered an injection of Narcan for him—please administer it immediately—I want to stay and watch."

Helen bustled out of the room, returned with the syringe, and gave her patient the shot.

Mr. Jackson opened his eyes, clapped his hands, and laughed. "Hey, everybody!" he said. "You guys trying to start the party without me?"

Hallway of a Thousand Screams

When our RNs came on shift at 7:00 a.m., they visited each of their five patients and wrote their name and five-digit phone number on the patient's whiteboard.

"This is my direct line," they said. "Just pick up your phone, dial this number, and your call will go straight to me."

Then they showed patients how to push the call button on their TV remotes.

"Pushing this button is another way to reach me, but any clerk, nurse, or CNA might answer, and then they'll have to call me. The fastest way to get in touch is to call my direct number."

When patients pushed their call buttons, a light came on outside of their rooms, and their calls also rang call light phones at each nurse's station. Everyone hated answering these calls because the sound quality was so poor—the volume was deafening, while the patient's words were almost always lost in static, requiring the person answering the call to walk to that patient's room to ask what she needed.

Malmed Memorial constantly skimped on investing in quality equipment, and this phone system was a prime example. Basically, we could tell which patient in which room was calling us, but we couldn't speak to her over the phone, which was ridiculous.

Our patients fell into three categories when it came to communicating that they needed assistance. A small percentage actually called their nurses directly. A much larger percentage pressed their call lights, initiating the time-consuming runaround I just described. And perhaps a nearly equal percentage left their doors open and screamed for help at any passerby, whether they were doctors, nurses, CNAs, clerks, physical therapists, dieticians, housekeepers, or other staff.

Everyone hated walking past those open doors. Often, we were on an urgent mission for another patient, or we'd been granted a morning or lunch break we had to use or lose. The patients yelled at us as long as we were visible to them. During this process, we typically heard the following:

"Get in here—I need help, *now*!"

"Where's my fuckin' nurse?"

"Don't you dare walk by!"

"Thanks for not stopping, asshole!"

Of course, we immediately assisted these patients if we were not performing an urgent task, even if they hadn't been assigned to us, but their constant shouting was one of the elements that added to the toxic atmosphere.

Once, while I was charting at Nurse Station 2, an entire hallway was comprised of patients screaming at staff through their open doors. A middle-aged blonde visitor walked past me, shaking her head at the cacophony.

"God bless you caregivers," she said.

Alex

One gloomy Thursday, Carmen assigned me to sit with a twenty-two-year-old Chinese American patient named Alex, who'd had a rough life. He'd survived three cancerous brain tumors, the second leaving him blind. In addition, his mentally disturbed older brother shot him in the head and stabbed him in his right side, leaving an ugly scar. Alex said the bullet caused serious brain damage. He called his mother daily, and she came to see him once or twice a week, but he was homeless because it wasn't safe for him to live with his mother, since his homicidal brother often visited her.

When I first met Alex, he'd just been transferred from our psychiatric hospital to Malmed Memorial because he'd contracted sepsis, a systemic infection that can quickly prove fatal. Alex had been in the psychiatric hospital because he suffered from deep depression and often had suicidal thoughts and intentions. Eating constantly to comfort himself, he weighed about four-hundred pounds, and he told me he had a certain type of diabetes—he once peed three liters during my eight-hour shift, but he hadn't had anything to drink!

Finally, a permanent itchy rash covered Alex's back. He constantly asked his caregivers to apply skin lotion and hydro-cortisone cream and to scratch his back with our gloved hands or gently with a comb. This is not an approved medical procedure, but I perfected a way to scratch his back with a comb so that it satisfied his urge to scratch without aggravating his rash. Alex also asked his caregivers to keep his head shaved, since hair made his scalp itch fiercely.

Despite his depression, Alex enjoyed childhood delights, such as listening to Disney shows targeted at older children on TV or YouTube. He also loved listening to children's books, his favorite being *The Boxcar Children* by Gertrude Chandler Warner. Every day I sat with him, I lent him my cell phone and charger so he could listen to books and children's programs all day long, his beat-up Android lacking this capability.

Alex owned a braille typewriter and had the exceptional ability to create art for the nurses and CNAs he liked. He made me a picture of a teddy bear and a complex scene with clouds, sailboats, seagulls, the ocean, and the beach. For my wife, he created an intricate design of teddy bears and hearts and another piece with hearts inside of hearts.

Some might call Alex developmentally delayed, but I think he lived in a world of childhood fantasy because of brain damage, trauma, and mental illness.

One day, Alex said, "You and Susie are my favorite CNAs— you're the only ones who take good care of me."

"What's wrong with the other CNAs?" I asked.

"They won't talk with me, they don't want to lotion or scratch my back, they won't shave my head, and they never let me listen to their cell phones. Also, they don't like to help me with showers. You

84

and Susie are the only ones."

I was proud Alex thought I provided excellent care, and I felt a stronger connection to Susie—I didn't know her very well, but she seemed to share the same deep level of compassion I felt toward most patients.

I was surprised Alex hadn't mentioned Alicia, my favorite CNA in our unit. When I told her he felt ignored by some of the CNAs who sat with him, she said, "Sometimes you can't give him as much attention as he wants because the other patient in his room is much sicker and needs a lot of help. For example, the other day, his roommate was a helpless man with the mental state of a two-year-old. He needed constant care—I kept telling Alex to call out if he really needed me, but his roommate required almost all of my time and attention."

I believed this because I'd once been in this same position with one of Alex's roommates. Our unit had two two-patient rooms, and the charge nurses didn't hesitate to put two sitter patients in these double rooms sharing a single CNA sitter. If the roommates both required a lot of time and attention, their level of care suffered because their CNA couldn't be two places at once.

When a doctor ordered a one-on-one sitter for a patient, she intended that the patient be assigned a dedicated CNA sitter, but our director, Victor Chukwu, had no qualms about breaking the spirit of these orders if it saved him labor costs or any other expense. All of us CNAs believed Alex should've been in a single-patient room with a dedicated sitter.

One day soon after I met Alex, Carmen assigned me to sit with him again, saying, "He's extremely depressed today and has been asking for you."

When I entered his room, Alex was curled up in a fetal position.

"Hey, Alex," I said, sitting in the chair next to his bed. "How you doing?"

"Not so great," he said.

"I heard you're feeling kind of down," I said.

"Man, the night nurses here are so mean. So are some of the day nurses, especially Penny. I just wish you and Susie could be the only ones taking care of me. I'm really depressed."

"Alex, with that keen hearing of yours, you must know I sigh a lot."

"Yeah," he said. "What's *that* about?"

"Well, between you and me, I've got depression. I'm always a little depressed, but sometimes I get really depressed, maybe like the way you're feeling right now."

"What do you do?" he said.

"I just try to focus on the things I really enjoy until I snap out of it. For example, I like hanging out with my wife, hiking with my dog, playing guitar, swimming, and reading and writing. Also, tasty food helps."

Alex laughed. "That's hard to get around here."

"Well, at least your mom brings you home-cooked," I said.

Alex's roommate was low maintenance, so I tried to build him a perfect day. I shaved his head and then helped him to shower—I noticed his right leg and ankle were deformed, but I didn't know the medical cause. However, it was clear he couldn't walk for much distance. After his shower, we chatted for a long time. I felt very close to Alex, as if he were my son or a younger brother. Then he listened to children's books and Disney and anime shows on my cell phone until he fell into a long nap.

When he awoke near my punch-out time, he said, "Thanks for hanging out with me today. You really cheered me up."

"My pleasure, buddy."

"Have a safe trip home," he said. "See you tomorrow."

"See you tomorrow."

When I sat with Alex the next day, his mother came to visit. She was elderly with a kind face. I sat as far away from his bed as possible so they could have some privacy, but I could hear snatches of their conversation.

"Alex," his mother said. "I'm getting old. I won't always be here for you. You're going to be on your own eventually. You need to grow up and be a man. You have to learn how to survive in life when I'm gone. You have to stop being so childish and crazy."

I didn't hear Alex's reply. When his mother left, he seemed lost in thought for a few minutes. He never mentioned what he was thinking, but I speculated he probably was incapable of growing up and becoming independent the way his mother wished because he had so many strikes against him; I hoped I was wrong.

The next day, Alicia sat with Alex, but his roommate required constant care.

The following morning, Mama informed all of us during our huddle that Alex had attempted suicide the evening before. He'd complained that most of his caregivers ignored him. He asked that he only be assigned good caregivers, such as Susie and me. When this demand was not met, Alex seized a large pair of nail clippers his mother had brought him, popped them into his mouth, and attempted to swallow them. Two sheriff's deputies assigned to the hospital were summoned, and they fought with Alex for two hours before they finally removed the nail clippers from his mouth.

After I heard this terrible news, I rushed from our huddle to my assigned patient for the day, a woman who'd fallen and fractured her skull and experienced a brain bleed. She was impulsive and a high fall risk, often leaping out of bed without donning her safety helmet, and I wasn't allowed to leave her room.

Later that morning, two ambulance crew members wheeled Alex on a gurney toward the elevators. I correctly guessed they were transporting him back to the psychiatric hospital since we'd cured his sepsis. I couldn't leave my room to say goodbye, and I didn't want to shout at him, so I remained silent, feeling Alex carry away a little piece of my heart.

Flight Four: 2017

Busted Up, Bruised, and Spent

Shit Happens

After Alex was transferred to the psychiatric hospital, Carmen assigned me to sit in a double room with two sitter patients. Patient 1: Mr. Rodrigues, a drunk going through withdrawal and constantly attempting to escape (the healthcare terminology is "elope"). Patient 2: Mr. Connors, who bore an intestinal infection from a bacteria called clostridium difficile or C. diff. He suffered from abdominal cramps and frequent bouts of watery, foul-smelling diarrhea.

Under normal circumstances, Mr. Connors would have been placed in a single-patient isolation room because C. diff is highly contagious and spreads through contact. Nurses are required to protect themselves with gowns, gloves, and a thorough hand washing with soap and water after they remove their gloves—alcohol-based hand gels can kill virtually any virus or bacteria, but they're not effective against C. diff. And all medical equipment, such as vital sign machines, must be cleaned with bleach wipes. We must have been short on isolation rooms that day.

Mr. Rodrigues, the recovering alcoholic, was unpopular with the female nursing staff because, besides repeatedly trying to elope, he constantly tried to stroke their hair and caress their bottoms. As his sitter, I found I could keep him in the room using voice commands, even though he spoke very little English.

Around 10:00 a.m., two things happened at once. Mr. Connors had an outpouring of malodorous diarrhea in bed while Mr. Rodrigues grew agitated. At first, I felt my normal frustration at having to deal with two sitter patients at the same time, but then I focused on Mr. Rodrigues. RN Gloria and CNA Alicia had come into the room to take his vital signs, but they were now trying to block him with their bodies so he wouldn't run out of the room. He drew back his fist to punch Gloria in the face; almost instantly, I had him in a bear hug and forced him down onto his bed while he attempted to strike all three of us.

"I'll keep him down," I said. "You guys activate a Code Gray." A Code Gray means a violent person, and Security and deputy sheriffs respond to the call.

Beneath my hands, Mr. Rodrigues struggled with increasing desperation, as if he feared for his life or was temporarily psychotic.

Alicia shouted at Mr. Rodrigues in Spanish, and he replied.

She spoke to him again, and he nodded vigorously.

"Okay," Alicia said. "I understand what's going on. He can't stand the smell of poop. I just made a deal with him. If we let him sit in a chair outside the room until the bad smell is gone, he won't try to run away."

"You sure?" I asked.

"Yes, it's okay," she said. "Let him go."

I released Mr. Rodrigues, and he hurried out of the room and, true to his word, sat in a chair Alicia fetched for him.

Urban Legend

When I came to work at Malmed Memorial in 2013, there was a supposedly true story going around about a patient running a drug and prostitution ring out of his room on the fifth floor.

This story has long since gone out of circulation, but I'll repeat it here because it's intriguing and just might be true.

As the story goes, a morbidly obese pimp and drug dealer named Marty X. was rushed into the emergency room with multiple gunshot wounds. His doctors worked at a feverish pace to patch him up and save his life. They succeeded. When his condition stabilized, his doctors transferred him to the less-acute fifth floor for a long recovery. As his health improved, hospital staff observed a steady stream of prostitutes and drug dealers flowing in and out of his room with large amounts of cash ending up in Marty's hands.

When it became undeniably clear Marty was continuing his illicit activities from his hospital bed, several doctors, nurses, and administrators told him to shut down operations while at Malmed. Marty refused, and these staffers applied increasing pressure on him to cease and desist.

Finally, Marty told them, "I'm tired of you assholes trying to interfere with my business. I've taken out a contract on each of you. I'm shutting *you* down."

Convinced these threats were real, these staffers rented a succession of cars and shuffled around obscure parking places until Marty eventually left the hospital.

Three years of peace ensued.

Then a severely overweight man with multiple gunshot wounds came in through the emergency room. As the doctors and nurses worked on him, they recognized this was the same Marty X. who'd threatened their lives. As the story goes, these workers continued to follow proper medical procedures but slowed their pace until Marty X. died on the operating table.

Obsession

Now and then, our director, Victor Chukwu, or the entire hospital management staff, became obsessed with a certain policy. For example, a patient named Emily Fields came in through the emergency room with a perforated colon. Rumor had it that when our surgeon repaired this tear, he accidentally nicked a healthy part of her colon with his scalpel, creating another wound, but he didn't realize it, and he closed her up.

I don't know if this rumor is true, but Mrs. Fields was a very sick patient on our unit for months. She became famous for her scathing tongue. I don't know if this was her normal personality or if she was in high pain or furious with the hospital over her second wound (assuming the rumor was true and she knew she'd been harmed in surgery), but she gave off all the signals of a patient who intended to sue us and was searching for a way to build her case.

This was so apparent that Mama talked about her in one of our morning huddles.

"Listen, y'all," she said in her Georgia accent. "Please give her the red-carpet treatment and make her feel special and like we really care about her. Let's see if we can turn her around."

Staff asked Mrs. Fields every day if she'd like to bathe. She'd momentarily rouse herself out of her drugged stupor to decline. Mrs. Fields was capable of bathing herself, but we would have bathed her if she allowed it so we could ensure she was clean. Unfortunately, most or all the nurses and CNAs who offered her baths failed to chart she'd declined. (I feel lucky in this regard because I was not one of the involved parties since I rarely bathed female patients.)

One day, Mrs. Fields telephoned the California Department of Public Health to complain she hadn't received a bath in over a week. When CDPH investigators looked into her claim, they decided it was well-founded because our documentation didn't show her receiving baths or refusing them. Mrs. Fields successfully sued the hospital for negligence over her lack of baths.

After that, our director, Victor Chukwu, and his team went wild to bathe patients. CNAs and RNs were instructed to ask every patient during every shift if they would like to bathe or shower and have their bed linen changed. At the extreme, a patient could be bathed and have her linen changed three times within a twenty-four-hour period if she agreed to these services during each eight-hour CNA shift. We were instructed to chart all bathing and linen change information electronically as usual and then record the same information on paper in a binder labeled "Shower Log." We were reminded to always document patient refusals of these activities.

These instructions stayed in place for years.

One day, Alicia said, "I'm not filling out the shower log anymore. The electronic charting is what really counts, and I just don't have time—I'm too busy taking care of patients. Besides, who knows what they're doing with that shower log because I never see anyone looking at it."

I'd already made the same decision. We stopped filling out the shower log, and nobody appeared to care.

After a brief respite from management obsession, the entire hospital then fixated on preventing patient falls, especially those categorized as preventable. In general, this is an admirable and worthy goal, but this new safety program displayed some of the same earmarks of the bathing fixation.

Every patient was deemed at risk, and patients received canary yellow blankets with matching wristbands, socks, warning signs above their beds, and falling star magnets on their doorframes. Victor Chukwu, a.k.a. Fuck You Chuck, inspected patient rooms daily, then weekly. After a year, the hospital terminated the entire program without a word.

Ironically, two years later in 2019, hospital management, in a cost-savings effort, decided to remove CNA sitters from the rooms of high fall-risk patients. Immediately, people began dropping, including a patient in our SDU who broke her neck. The CNAs expected the hospital to reverse this reckless new policy, but it was still in place at the time of this writing. In fact, according to Rose Oni, the hospital, or at least our unit, was in the midst of a crisis regarding this situation. It's a bit disconcerting that our hospital administrators were unable to perceive simple cause and effect. If the hospital didn't want high fall-risk patients crashing to the floor, it should've assigned them CNA sitters. Or at least researched how highly ranked hospitals prevented patient falls and implemented these best practices.

Back in 2017: shortly after the yellow-blanket fall prevention campaign ceased, Beretta Blowgun became obsessed with the refrigerator in our break room. This is not the first time our lunches had been under siege. As you'll recall, Victor used to toss out lunches that didn't smell fresh to him.

Beretta made a rule that we were no longer allowed to place our lunch bags in the refrigerator. This was frustrating because some of us carried multiple food items to work in a small vinyl or paper lunch bag. For example, I usually brought an apple, a yogurt, and a plastic container of leftovers in a small vinyl bag.

I didn't want these items exposed and loose in the refrigerator, especially since I'd had my lunch stolen twice. The bags typically placed in the refrigerator were not insulated, and we didn't want our food to spoil. Other staffers with insulated bags or giant backpacks containing food placed them on a large table across from the fridge.

Beretta never explained the reason for this new rule, and nurses, especially RNs working twelve-hour shifts, were terrified she'd pitch their lunches and they'd have to work hungry during their long day. The rumor was that two nurses angered Beretta by putting their large backpacks in the refrigerator. Instead of making a rule stating no oversized backpacks were allowed in the fridge, she apparently decided to ban *all* lunch bags.

However, Beretta's no lunch bag rule never caught on. Nobody fucked with our food!

4:23—Stupidity and Lowest Bidders

Our nearly brand-new hospital contained serious flaws. For example, some bathroom doors locked and others didn't. As you can imagine, we didn't want suicidal patients locking themselves in bathrooms. Also, some toilets had a flush handle while others used an electric eye. It's sad to see a sick and weak patient frantically feeling the rear of the toilet to determine how she can flush her bowel movement. All bathroom faucets were activated by an electric eye, so this unhappy pantomime was repeated, complicated by the fact that there was a tiny lever controlling whether the water flowed hot or cold—and one room had a faucet lacking *any* temperature control. I never encountered a patient who understood the purpose of this lever.

Finally, after the patient had washed her hands, she needed to activate an electric eye to receive a paper towel from the dispenser. And many times, the battery was dead, so the patient couldn't dry her hands unless there were washcloths or towels in her bedroom. I assumed all these electric-eye-activated devices were meant to save water and paper and maximize hand hygiene.

However, imagine you're suffering from any number of ailments—perhaps you've got a migraine, or you're highly nauseous, or you're extremely ill from chemotherapy. You can hardly walk, and it's a major effort to get to the bathroom. After you've done your business, you have to play guessing games with the toilet, the faucet, and the paper towel dispenser. If you have a CNA sitter, she will explain how things work or activate the electric eyes for you. God help you if you're on your own.

Worse, from the back of each bathroom door, a long, sharp bolt protruded at the forearm level (for a person such as me who's 5'11'') that constantly cut and bruised patients and staff as they entered or left the bathrooms. I assumed this bolt had been placed there to accommodate some kind of coat hanger requirement for handi-capped people, which is fine, in principle. Still, given the amount of injury these bolts caused, one would hope the hospital would replace them with some type of less dangerous hook, but I doubt this will ever happen.

The bathroom designs frustrated nurses as well. A standard issue in hospital bathrooms is a mini shower head connected to the toilet. Let's say a patient has just had a bowel movement in a bedpan. Then the nurse can wash the stool into the toilet with the mini shower head and rinse out the bedpan until it's clean and reusable. However, virtually none of the toilets in our hospital was equipped with a mini shower head. Therefore, every time a patient had a bowel movement in a bedpan, we had to pitch the whole thing into the trash, which is malodorous, unsanitary, and wasteful.

The showers represented another dangerous design fault. When the new hospital opened, none of the showers in patient bathrooms had a lip at the base to hold in the water. As a result, the bathrooms and patient rooms flooded, creating not only a mess but a slick-floor fall danger. Until workmen installed these lips, our unit had a CNA working full time cleaning up the floods from patient showers.

Some of the design failings wasted time and proved ineffective. In the old hospital, nurses could control each patient's room temperature from the in-room thermostat—imagine a chilled patient in one room and a feverish patient in another. This was an expedient arrangement. But, as it stood now, if we wanted to adjust room temperature, we had to phone Engineering, which may or may not have resolved the issue.

Also, our time-keeping system was defective. I once sat with a schizophrenic patient who was highly agitated because the time on his room clock never changed—he was desperate to see time passing. When I called Engineering and asked them to put a new battery in his clock, an engineer informed me all room clocks were hard-wired for electricity and were supposed to be in synch with a master clock, even though they weren't. I also learned the new time-keeping system was both very expensive and riddled with bugs.

Weeks later, that patient left, the clock in his room still frozen at 4:23, and I often saw clocks in patient rooms displaying the wrong time. In CNA school, our instructor frequently reminded us of the importance of keeping patients oriented to month, date, year, day of week, and time of day. Patients, we were instructed, should always have access to an accurate clock.

And our hospital failed to accommodate younger-generation patients who had no interest in television; two of their primary sources of entertainment were YouTube and Pandora. Our nurses, including me, constantly lent these patients our smart phones so they could keep themselves entertained, especially mentally ill patients who acted out when they were bored. But this was inconvenient for the nurses, and it would've been much better if our hospital could've provided patients with access to these applications.

To sum up my feelings toward our hospital design, I turn to

astronaut John Glenn as he climbed aboard an Atlas rocket on a NASA launch pad in 1962: "I felt exactly how you would feel if you were getting ready to launch and knew you were sitting on top of two million parts—all built by the lowest bidder on a government contract."[1]

Busted Up, Bruised, and Spent[2]

A vital sign machine takes blood pressure, pulse, blood oxygen saturation percentage, and temperature—readings critical to health, even survival. Sometimes when RNs and CNAs collected vital signs, we had to switch machines several times before we found one that was fully functional. Of our unit's ten vital sign machines, at any given time at least half were broken. Sometimes virtually all were out of commission.

Often, the nozzle that connects with the small hose on the blood pressure cuff was missing, which meant the device couldn't read pulse or blood pressure. Also, the nozzles on our machines had been reconfigured to fit a new type of blood pressure cuff the hospital adopted. The new, jury-rigged nozzles lacked a safety feature keeping them from over-inflating, so twice I witnessed patients screaming in agony as their cuffs over-squeezed their arms. Also, sometimes our equipment could collect blood pressure but failed to take a pulse.

Additionally, vital sign machines have a pulse-ox finger clip measuring both pulse and blood oxygen saturation levels. Often these finger clips were missing—I don't know why, but there appeared to be a black market for them because they'd been stolen in large quantities ever since I came onboard at the hospital.

The final device on vital sign equipment is the thermometer. About half of our vital sign machines employed a standard oral thermometer, and only about half of these worked. The other machines used a forehead-scanning temporal thermometer. These were by far the most popular with patients and staff because they were fast and non-invasive. Unfortunately, the batteries in these scanners were often dead.

One day, it was time for me to take 11:00 a.m. vital signs. I examined every vital sign machine in the storage room. The most functional one was capable only of taking blood pressure and pulse, so that's the one I used. I tried to compensate for the broken device by feeling patients' wrists for temperature and looking for any visible signs of low blood oxygen saturation, which included asking patients if they felt nauseous, dizzy, light-headed, weak, or had a headache.

When I entered Mr. Valdez's room, his RN, Benny Soto, charted at the computer. Benny was a new nurse; he was a handsome guy with a crew cut, and he had one of the quickest and most joyful smiles I'd ever seen. He was hands-down the most cheerful nurse on our unit, a real ray of light, but I'd been a bit worried about him. His smile came less often now, and his expression often looked stressed and strained. Since I was sixty and he was in his twenties, I'd been planning to ask him father-to-son-style if he wanted to talk about what was bothering him.

While thinking about this, I took Mr. Valdez's blood pressure and pulse, apologizing for the machine's limited capabilities.

Benny shook his head in disgust. "Do what you gotta do," he said. "I can never find one that works, either." We left the room at the same time, closing Mr. Valdez's door behind us.

"Benny," I said softly. "Is this place getting to you?"

"I'll tell you what gets to me the most," he said. "It's how we get treated by a lot of our patients. They don't want to be helped, they hate us, and they say terrible things to us, and we're not allowed to say anything back. You can tell at a glance that a patient's hostile and doesn't want any care—as far as I'm concerned, they're wasting precious beds that should go to patients who'll actually let us help them get better. I just didn't expect to have so many low-rent patients."

"Welcome to Malmed Memorial!" I said.

Shortly after this conversation, Benny resigned and accepted a position at another local hospital, one of the nation's best.

Forgiveness

One morning, we admitted a patient who'd destroyed his liver and kidneys from drinking. Mr. Scofield also suffered from a raft of additional medical problems. When I entered his room to take vital signs, he spoke to me.

"It's okay if you take my vital signs," he said. "But I'm refusing all further treatment. I've been an alcoholic all my life, and I've deeply hurt everyone I've ever cared about. I just want to die."

I finished taking his vital signs, but paused in his room, not sure what to say.

"I really need to talk to someone," he said.

"I'd be happy to listen," I said.

Tears streamed down his face. "What would you do if you were me?" he asked.

I thought for a moment. "Call those I've hurt, apologize, and ask for forgiveness."

"God, that would feel so good," he said. "But I'm afraid they'll reject my apology."

"I'd still try it," I said, thinking about how badly I wished my parents had called me, admitted to the child abuse, apologized for it, explained it, and asked for my forgiveness.

"Okay," he said. "Would you please stay with me while I make the first call?" I nodded.

He dialed a number on his cell phone. I heard a woman's voice on the other end of the line, and Mr. Scofield issued a short but heart-felt apology.

Whatever she said made him smile and cry at the same time.

Two weeks later, Mr. Scofield died a peaceful and forgiven man.

Two-Patient Hell-Hole Room

Although our director, Victor Chukwu, was forced to eliminate four-patient sitter rooms in the old hospital, our new hospital had two two-patient rooms on each medical/surgical unit. If only one patient in these rooms was a sitter, this worked out fine. But if both patients were sitters, these could become two-patient hell-hole rooms. For example, shortly after Mr. Scofield died, I sat in one of these rooms with Mr. Washington and Mr. Burns.

Mr. Washington was an eighty-five-year-old with bladder cancer that had spread to (at least) his liver, lower spine, and brain. He was unable to stand or walk. Sometimes he slept or rested quietly, but he often whimpered and whined for long periods, his words virtually incomprehensible, while his brown eyes resembled those of a desperate, abused puppy begging for mercy.

So, a sitter for Mr. Washington, a total-care patient, needed to alert his nurse every time he was anxious, agitated, in pain, or frantically attempting to climb out of bed. We also needed to keep him calm and reassure and prevent him from yanking out his IVs or Foley catheter. In addition, we had to empty his Foley bag, measure his output, and clean him and change his linens if he had a bowel movement. Then, of course, there were the basics, like bathing him, feeding him, providing oral and Foley care, and charting his information.

Mr. Washington should have had a dedicated one-on-one sitter, which is what his doctor ordered. Unfortunately, his roommate, Mr. Burns, was an extremely demanding patient, and it was difficult for a single CNA sitter to take proper care of both patients at the same time.

We treated Mr. Burns for prostate and bone cancer. He spewed curses, threats, and insults at his nurses and CNAs during all of his waking moments.

He liked to say, "Don't get comfortable because I'm going to work you hard, man!"

A couple of hours into my shift, Mr. Washington called out on the other side of the room. "I've got to catch the bus!" He whipped his long legs over the side rails of his bed. I got to him just in time to calm him, put his legs back in bed, and call out to his nurse to let her know he probably needed pain medicine—two-patient sitter rooms are located near nurses' stations. Mr. Washington was well over six feet tall with long arms and legs and giant, spidery hands. It was scary how quickly he could launch himself out of bed.

When I turned to check on Mr. Burns, he'd taken off his hospital gown, flipped onto his stomach, and slid his feet to the floor before getting stuck in that position.

"Help!" he cried. "I need help!"

Mr. Burns was wildly jealous of his roommate and frequently pulled stunts like this if I needed to care for Mr. Washington.

I summoned Penny, who was at the nurses' station.

"Allen," she said. "How could you let this happen?"

"Sorry," I said. "I was preventing Mr. Washington from getting out of bed and falling. I can't be two places at once."

We put Mr. Burns back to bed and got him back into his gown.

After Penny left, he said, "I've got friends. We're going to get you alone and beat the shit out of you!"

Suddenly, I became angry. Even though the charge nurse is supposed to rotate our assignments, I'd been sitting with Mr. Burns for two weeks—male CNAs often were assigned the most hostile and challenging patients; also Mr. Burns demanded that all female nurses strip naked for him—and I was sick of his bad behavior. My dislike for him bordered on hatred. I didn't take his threat seriously, but I wanted to get him into as much trouble as possible, hoping that somehow his doctors and nurses could get him under better control or we could discharge him or transfer him to another facility sooner.

When Mr. Burns and Mr. Washington both fell asleep, I walked out of the room to the nurses' station.

"Mr. Burns threatened to have his friends beat me up," I told Penny.

Penny, Virginia Black, and Carla Kilgore burst out laughing.

"What's so funny?" I asked.

"You don't take this threat seriously, do you?" said Penny.

"No," I said. "But I thought we were supposed to report threats."

"Honey," Carla said. "Mr. Burns' cancer has metastasized to his brain. He's totally crazy. He can't help his behavior."

I'd looked up Mr. Burns' diagnosis several times: prostate cancer, bone cancer. No doctor or nurse had ever clued me in that he had brain cancer. My anger melted, and I felt great empathy for Mr. Burns.

When I returned to his room, he was awake, shivering intensely, a frequent occurrence. I retrieved a blanket from the warmer and spread it over him.

"God bless you for taking such good care of me," he said.

9, 14, 28

When I first worked the floor on my unit, I was responsible for nine patients. I'd bring each one ice water and then ask my patients if they wanted bath supplies or for me to change the linens on their beds. I'd also offer to assist patients with a bed bath or shower if they needed help. During the day, I could cycle through these rooms multiple times, and I'd punch out at the end of my shift feeling satisfied all of my patients had their needs met during the eight hours I cared for them.

Then the short staffing began. Floor CNAs were put in charge of 14 patients each, and I had to struggle to meet all their needs, which was nearly or fully impossible. Some days, I went home feeling guilty because I hadn't even seen some of the patients who'd been in my charge, having been forced to focus my time on only my most sick and demanding patients.

Later, it was common for a single CNA to work the floor, caring for all 28 patients on our unit, provided there even *was* a floor CNA—many times, all CNAs were assigned to sitter patients. When I was on the floor with 28 patients, I passed ice water and then answered call lights and responded to RN requests for patient care. This ate up my entire day. I never had time to go room to room and ask patients what I could do for them. I had to train myself to not feel bad about this because my workload was beyond my control. When I got home at night, I told myself I worked hard and tried my best to care for as many patients as I could.

Although CNAs were at the bottom of the nursing food chain, I had at least some idea why our hospital experienced increased short staffing. For one thing, our CEO had announced expenses were exceeding revenue and cuts would be hitting our already-shoestring budget. Second, the number of sitter patients in our care had been increasing. Third, as baby boomers age and become sick, they are flooding our nation's healthcare systems. The number of people with multiple chronic conditions is expected to grow from 8.7 million at the time of this writing to almost 37 million in 2030.[3] These conditions include diabetes, arthritis, asthma, depression, hypertension, Alzheimer's, and lung disease.[4]

And, according to one of my CNA continuing education class instructors, Michelle Downy, healthcare facilities, such as hospitals, have to decide how to handle the deluge of mentally ill and dementia (including Alzheimer's) patients entering the system. Is it best to group these patients into psychiatric and memory care units or distribute them among the general population? Malmed Memorial had neither of these units, so each psychiatric and dementia patient was placed in the general population and received a dedicated, one-on-one CNA sitter, which was labor-intensive, expensive, disruptive, and often dangerous.

Personally, I'd prefer to see these patients in specialty units designed to best meet their needs. This also would minimize the high level of disruption these patients cause other patients and staff when they're mixed with the general population. For example, we once had an aggressive dementia patient who liked to wander; she wasn't sedated or restrained, and it was impossible to keep her in her bed or room. Also, she presented a constant elopement risk.

Ideally, a patient like this would be housed in a locked memory care facility in which she could roam without endangering her safety or the safety of others. Our patient was supposed to stay in Room 18, but she assaulted a family member of the patient in Room 5 who'd just stepped out into the hall. Up to four nurses at a time repeatedly herded or dragged her away from Room 5, where a lawsuit awaited us if she attacked anyone associated with that room again.

School Day

One sunny morning, I sat with an advanced dementia patient named Harold Baker, who was seventy and built like a trim and muscular basketball player. Mr. Baker's eyes were so wide open they looked like those of a horror movie character viewing a terrifying monster.

Suddenly, Mr. Baker conversed with his invisible granddaughter. "What's that, honey?" he said. "You need me to take you to school?"

Mr. Baker went berserk. He leaped to his feet and lunged for the door, despite his crippled limbs. I caught him before he fell and guided him back to bed, with him blaring, "I've got to get Emma to school! Get your fucking hands off me!"

Even though I'd lowered Mr. Baker back into the bed, suddenly he was all fists and kicking feet. He drove a foot into my right shin and punched my right wrist. Blood dripped down my arm from a deep, three-inch jagged scratch. I opened the door and called for help.

While I held him down, I reflected on how much I disliked caring for patients who were out-of-control and couldn't be reasoned with, especially when they weren't sedated or restrained.

These patients needed compassionate and quality care, which I believe could best be provided in specialty facilities designed to best meet their needs—I even accepted a job once to care for dementia patients in a memory care facility, but I failed the physical because I had a temporarily strained rotator cuff.

I thought about how terrible it would be to have an altered mental status. I believe I have a sharp mind, and I'd be in living hell if I lost it. My father had advanced dementia aggravated by several strokes. He declined from a skilled pianist and voracious reader to a mute and incontinent near-vegetable who tore up his beloved books and constantly threw household belongings off the front porch onto the lawn below. When he grew violent, my mother placed him in a memory care facility, where he received excellent care and was calm and content.

I also thought about how ferocious patients become when they believe we're preventing them from performing a task that was once critical for them, such as getting to work on time or shepherding a child to or from school, especially since we were located in one of the most dangerous spots in the United States.

A few minutes after my cry for help, Penny entered the room with two RNs in tow.

"Hold him down, you guys," she said. "I have a doctor's order here for Haldol (a brand name for the anti-psychotic medicine haloperidol, which, among other things, reduces agitation)."

The RNs immobilized a powerful leg each while I firmly held each of Mr. Baker's thick wrists. Penny injected his right arm with the Haldol. Then everyone let him go and jumped back.

Mr. Baker was furious, but he remained in bed, cursing us.

"Allen," Penny said. "Keep him under control without getting hurt. I'll check on him in a little while. Hopefully, the Haldol will kick in soon."

Mr. Baker received the injection at noon. He attempted to jump out of bed and elope for the next hour and a half. Then Alicia relieved me for lunch, and Mr. Baker continued this behavior. When I returned at 2:00 p.m., Mr. Baker was just beginning to get drowsy. He slept from 2:30 p.m. until 3:00 p.m.

Around 2:55, Penny looked into the room. "He asleep?" she asked.

"Just fell asleep at 2:30," I said.

She shook her head in wonder. Depending on the patient, Haldol works immediately, or on a delay, or not at all. We were lucky to receive an hour of calm and sleep from Mr. Baker.

When he woke up, he was full-bore back into escape mode. Fortunately, I kept him in bed without getting injured. When I was supposed to punch out at 3:30 p.m., the hallway and nurses' station outside his room were empty of staff; I imagined tumbleweeds blowing by. I had no way to call Penny or the charge nurse, so I waited to be relieved. Mr. Baker's agitation and level of violence rose toward his next eruption.

At 3:50 p.m., Beretta Blowgun came into the room and reprimanded me. "Why are you still here?" she said. "Why didn't you call someone to relieve you?"

"Because sitters aren't allowed to have phones," I said. "And this patient isn't allowed one, either. And nobody was at the front desk or in the hall."

"Go punch out!" she said. "I'll take over here. How much trouble could this patient be?"

Respite

Shortly after my final encounter with Mr. Baker, my wife, Elizabeth, and I vacationed for a week in Santa Barbara. After we checked into our Airbnb around 6:00 p.m., we walked along State Street, looking for a restaurant in which to eat dinner.

"I'm in the mood for a place with white tablecloths and live guitar music," Elizabeth said. She possesses a deep love of music, a passion she shares with her father and me, and her tastes include rock, blues, country, jazz, opera, and classical tunes. And she particularly enjoys live shows because her rough childhood caused her to grow up believing she didn't deserve to attend concerts.

As a teen, she often cranked up the volume on her record player, but her parents inevitably silenced her. When she started dating me and encountered her first high-quality stereo system, she played her CDs so loud that she blew out my beloved speakers. Did she learn her lesson? Yes—she discovered she enjoyed listening to her music at high volume. The speakers in my blue Ford Ranger pick-up were the next to die.

Almost immediately, we passed a cozy-looking bistro. Through its open door, we saw and heard a guitar player sitting on a stool at the front of the eatery, facing tables covered with white tablecloths that were rapidly filling up with tanned and hungry diners.

"Oh my God," my wife exclaimed. "This is like magic."

As our waitress seated us, I vowed to keep our visit romantic and enchanted. No talk or brooding about Mr. Baker, Beretta Blowgun, or any other denizens of Malmed Memorial. Elizabeth must have made a similar vow because she never mentioned the head veterinary technician who frequently bullied her or any other aspect of her stressful job.

We spent seven relaxing days frequenting museums; the local zoo, where we hand-fed a giraffe; a renovated industrial district offering live music and wine tasting in settings such as a former auto repair garage; and other unique and intriguing destinations.

The highlight of our trip was a whale-watching expedition during which we were awed by several solitary humpback whales breaching salt and pepper, slapping the water with their flippers, and spouting white spray. As we journeyed from one whale to another, we encountered four separate pods of silver-slick bottlenose dolphins with about fifty members each frolicking in the azure water and surfing our bow wake, a recurring vision of grace.

Asshole, Amplified

Back from our refreshing vacation, which had given Elizabeth and me a blissful glimpse into the promised land of retirement and leisure, I sat with Mr. Burns, the brain cancer patient who'd insulted and threatened me all day and then eventually thanked me for covering him with a heated blanket.

He continued to scream curses, insults, and threats at his CNA sitters at full volume during every moment, unless he was eating or sleeping.

One of his favorite expressions was, "Come here, you stupid motherfucker and hurry up or I'll beat the shit out of you!"

In addition, he'd been refusing his medications. Thank goodness for CNA's safety's sake, he couldn't stand or walk. He was more obnoxious than ever, and he had a one-track mind about eloping— he frequently tried to climb out of bed, which was guaranteed to result in a fall—and getting him back into bed was more challenging, since he'd started hitting and kicking his sitters.

You might be thinking Mr. Burns was a normal guy who'd been struck with brain cancer that turned him into a mean-spirited person. However, I don't think this is the case. I've learned in several continuing education classes about Alzheimer's and dementia that these diseases can magnify the patient's natural personality. For example, happy people become happier while mean people become meaner.

This was certainly the case with my father. Before his dementia manifested, he was self-centered, inconsiderate, angry, cruel, and violent (the latter when my brother Danny and I were children). After dementia struck, he refused to wear his hearing aids, even though he was nearly deaf. He made virtually no effort to communicate with our mother, let alone other family members. He just holed up in his study reading and working on self-directed projects. When our mother needed to speak with him, she'd talk to him in a raised voice. Invariably, she failed to speak loudly enough. When she raised her voice a notch higher, our father would bellow at her that she was hurting his ears.

After one such occurrence, our mother stormed off to the kitchen to prepare dinner, and our father allowed me to see a look of utter hatred in his eyes while he pointed after our mother and gleefully gestured strangling her to death. This was the same look Danny and I saw as children, right before our father beat the bejesus out of us, often for no reason. Our father eventually attempted to trip our eighty-eight-year-old mother, and that's when she put him into a memory care facility.

But back to Mr. Burns. Whenever his daughter Luca came to visit, she and her father fell into epic shouting matches. It was clear Mr. Burns had been yelling at Luca all her life, and he'd turned her into a seething monster. A Care Management staffer confided in me that she'd learned from Mr. Burns' aunt, the matriarch of the family, that he and his daughter were drug addicts who were irrational and constantly fighting.

When I sat with Mr. Burns on this occasion, night-shift CAN, Jane, warned me he was off his meds, more agitated and offensive than ever, and combative.

Sure enough, when I entered his room, he said, "Oh for fuck's sake, I have to put up with a stupid motherfucker like you all day?"

This behavior continued for another hour or two. Then Mr. Burns said, "Hey, stupid motherfucker, help me to the bathroom so I can pee, and hurry up, or I'll beat the shit out of your dumb ass!"

"Mr. Burns," I said. "You have a Foley catheter. Just go ahead and pee, and your pee will go into the urine collection bag."

"You dumb fuck!" he screamed. "Stop lying to me! I need to pee in the bathroom *now*, and I'm going to do it whether your stupid ass helps me or not!"

I tried to reason with him, but he shouted more insults so loudly he couldn't hear a word I said.

Suddenly, he swung his lame legs over the bed rail, planted his feet on the floor, and prepared to launch himself toward the bathroom door. I knew this move would result in a serious fall.

Just before he did so, I grabbed his ankles and flipped his legs back into the bed, expecting him to punch me in the face at any moment. He went berserk and yelled louder than ever.

"You stupid motherfucker!" he shouted. "That's abuse! Wait until I tell my family! We'll ruin you!"

Gloria, Mr. Burns' nurse, heard him shouting and came to see what was going on.

"What happened?" she said.

"Mr. Burns is confused," I said. I explained what I'd done, and why. "He thinks I was too rough."

"You lying motherfucker!" Mr. Burns said.

Gloria whispered, "Thanks. You did the right thing."

Our charge nurse, Carla Kilgore, who'd also heard the commotion, arrived, and I repeated my story. She shook her head in disgust at Mr. Burns' behavior.

"You couldn't let him fall," she said. "What else could you do? Don't worry, you're in the clear."

A couple of hours later, Luca entered Mr. Burns' room, where I was still sitting.

"How you doing, Daddy?" she said.

"This stupid motherfucker abused me," he said.

Luca shot me a look of hatred, walked to the nearest nurses' station, picked up a phone, and said to the hospital operator, "I need to report elder abuse."

I found Carla Kilgore at the front nurses' station and told her about Luca's complaint.

"I'll talk to her," she said, rising to her feet.

Since Luca was with her father, I no longer had to sit with him. I decided to eat lunch. As I was finishing, Carla came into the break room.

"How'd it go?" I said.

"I couldn't reason with her," she said. "That girl and her father are both crazy and just want to scream at everyone. She's definitely reporting you, but don't worry, nothing with come of it."

"Really?" I said.

"Yes, we get accused of stuff like this all the time, and there's never any evidence to back it up. You need to fill out an occurrence report. Put in everything you can about Mr. Burns' confusion, bad behavior, and constant efforts to climb out of bed."

Even though Carla reassured me, I shook from an overload of adrenaline. I felt as if I'd just been in a car wreck, and I had little ability to concentrate. I couldn't imagine effectively filling out the user-unfriendly online occurrence report, although I knew it was urgent I do so as soon as possible. Then I remembered something. A psychiatrist had prescribed medications for anxiety, depression, and insomnia I took every night at bedtime.

After my first ultra-stressful day caring for Mr. Burns, I placed a Klonopin anti-anxiety pill in the glove compartment of my silver Honda for some future date. I absolutely don't believe in people, especially in healthcare, working under the influence of drugs or alcohol, but I knew I wasn't functional without taking the Klonopin, and I also knew it wouldn't make me high—it would just cause my anxiety to disappear and clear my thoughts. I slipped down to my car in the parking garage and took the pill.

I spent a couple of hours filling out the report, and I felt calm and relaxed by the time I finished it. I used the rest of my shift to care for "normal" patients, then punched out, drove the hour home, and sipped a couple of margaritas upon my arrival. Welcome to Malmed Memorial!

The next day, as I worked the floor, an ambulance crew wheeled a discharged Mr. Burns down the hall on a gurney toward the elevators and exit. Several staffers with kinder hearts than mine called out goodbyes. I turned away.

Flight Five: 2018

Renewal

The Customer's Always Right

According to a division of *U.S. News and World Report* that tracks hospitals, our patients, after discharge, gave Malmed Memorial an overall satisfaction rating of 3 stars out of 5. We also received 3-star satisfaction marks in the following categories: willingness to recommend the hospital, doctors' communications, nurses' communications, pain relief, efforts to prevent medication harm, quality of discharge information, and noise volume.

We received 2-star scores for involvement in recovery, staff responsiveness, and room cleanliness.

We didn't receive 4-star or 5-star evaluations in any category.

This confirmed my observations that our level of care appeared average, not great. Although, to be fair, one should factor in that many of our patients were low-income, poorly educated, chronically ill, and often angry about these circumstances. Some patients bitterly complained if our level of service didn't match that of a five-star hotel! It's hard to know exactly the truth.

From my viewpoint, our doctors appeared to be competent and compassionate. I'd rarely seen a doctor mistreat a patient, and I'd seen them demonstrate great kindness when comforting a patient or a loved one or explaining that a patient's condition had become terminal with no remaining treatment options. My main issue with our doctors was they constantly sent us combative, mentally ill patients with no orders for sedatives or restraints that would greatly improve patient and staff safety.

As for our nurses, I've already mentioned some were responsive and compassionate while others could be cruel or indifferent to their patients, sometimes treating them as if they were simply pieces of meat.

And we had one nurse on our unit, Tammy, who I suspected was incompetent. I overheard she'd been placed on probation twice for making mistakes in which another nurse prevented her from causing harm to a patient. I once sat with one of her patients who was in severe pain. She gave him a painkiller at 10:00 a.m. and told him she'd return with another one in four hours, at 2:00 p.m. When she hadn't come back at 2:00 p.m. and her patient awoke in agony at 3:00 p.m., I called her and asked her to bring the patient another pill.

"I'm coming," she said.

A few minutes later, she stuck her head into the room and said, "I'm sorry, Mr. Hamilton. I'll bring your pain meds as soon as it's due, but we still have to wait another hour."

Behind her, Carla Kilgore said, "Please get him something immediately."

Maybe that's one reason many of the staff liked to say, "If I ever get sick, I'm *never* coming here."

In addition, there was a strong vibe at Malmed that upper management was evil. For example, twenty employees from a horribly managed department, after complaining for more than two years without resolution, marched to the office of the highest executive to whom they reported, chanting, "Meet with us."

Not only did the executive decline the meeting, but he locked himself in his office and ordered deputy sheriffs to disperse his staff!

Chaos

Our charge nurse, Carmen Sanchez, seemed comfortable with a high level of chaos I found frustrating and disconcerting, especially for an acute care environment. Or maybe it's just that she was a poor manager. For example, I once arrived at our morning huddle on time and listened to all the announcements while examining the day's assignment sheet. We had five CNAs on our unit, with four of them appearing to be real sitters while I was a "fake sitter" who actually would be working the floor.

A word about fake sitters. Because Malmed was often short-staffed, the Staffing Office was very stingy about assigning CNAs to various units. However, it was obligated to provide CNAs for sitter patients. So if our unit had two real sitter patients, but it also wanted two CNAs to work the floor, our unit gamed the system by falsifying our assignment sheet to show we had four sitter patients instead of two.

This falsified assignment sheet was then passed out to the nurses and CNAs in our morning huddle. The CNAs couldn't know which of us were real versus fake sitters, and this was virtually never clarified by Carmen or Mama, the two charge nurses who alternated conducting these beginning of shift get-togethers.

I ended many a meeting by asking, "Can you please tell us who the real and fake sitters are?" It was only then that all was revealed. I grew weary of asking this question every day, so sometimes I just went to the room where I was supposedly sitting to find out if there was a CNA sitter there waiting to be relieved. If there wasn't one, I knew I was working the floor.

So after our early morning meeting, I began working the floor. I was familiar with the patient I'd been assigned, and I knew he was a mellow guy with dementia who was a fake sitter patient.

However, after the huddle ended, Carmen realized one sitter she thought was a patient care technician was actually a CNA, which meant she could be assigned to take vital signs at 11:00 a.m. PCT's were not allowed to take vital signs. Carmen flagged down Alicia in the hall and told her the revised vital sign assignments, while Alicia grilled her until she figured out who were the real and fake sitters. Alicia assumed Carmen would deliver this information to the other four CNAs and especially to me as the senior-most CNA on our unit, but she didn't. Just to clarify, Carmen made changes to the already inaccurate assignment sheet and then told only Alicia.

Chaos ensued.

For my part, based on the incorrect information on the assignment sheet, I passed ice water to the wrong patients, helped the wrong patients with baths and bed linen changes, and almost took vital signs for the wrong patients. This meant nobody was taking care of my assigned patients. Finally, Alicia saw I was about to take vital signs in incorrect rooms and brought me up to speed on what was going on. She was amazed Carmen hadn't already done so, but I wasn't surprised. So I took vital signs for my assigned patients and finally managed between 2:30 p.m. and punch out time at 3:30 p.m. to help these patients with baths and linen changes.

In other words, thanks to Carmen's ineptitude, it took me four hours to clarify my assignment and another four hours to complete what amounted to eight hours of work.

Magnet Repelled

Shortly after the so-called day of chaos, Malmed Memorial's CEO announced expenses were exceeding revenue and appropriate action would be taken to address this issue. One tangible result was a thinning out of the hospital's senior ranks. Victor Chukwu was forced out and went to share his questionable management skills with another local hospital.

Also, a couple of years previously, Malmed hired a supposed superstar named Sally Campfield as the chief nursing executive. One mission was to achieve magnet status for the hospital's nursing operations. Awarded by the American Nurses' Credentialing Center (ANCC), an affiliate of the American Nurses Association, magnet status indicates a hospital successfully has met all of the criteria measuring the strength and quality of an outstanding nursing program. As of this writing, magnet status had been granted to only 8% of the hospitals in the U.S., including neighboring Stanford University Hospital & Clinics and UCSF Medical Center.[5] The improvements a hospital needs to make to achieve magnet status typically require over four years and $2 million.[6]

When Sally first arrived, the nurses and CNAs thought her

mission was impossible and she was destined to go down in flames; we were right. Sally left Malmed around the same time as Fuck You Chuck. I never noticed any improvements in our nursing operations I could trace back to her, since I hardly noticed any improvements at all, although she may have been the person to create the mandatory nursing huddles we attended when we came on shift at 7:00 a.m. In general, I liked these meetings and found them valuable.

I met Sally once when she first came on board. She was a fit, pin-striped, and petite African American woman with a lot of energy and drive. She introduced herself to a clump of us nurses working at Nurse Station 3 and asked us about our single greatest area of job dissatisfaction. Without hesitation, we all said the same thing: "short staffing."

"That's what virtually every nurse says," she said. "We'll have to see what we can do about that."

Two years later, our short staffing issue hadn't demonstrated the slightest improvement.

I don't have strong feelings either way about Sally leaving. On one hand, it's a shame she was hired by a mediocre hospital and assigned an impossible mission. On the other hand, I witnessed virtually no improvements under her reign, and there was a rumor she mistreated her staff.

In any event, the administration at Malmed certainly repelled Sally's attempts at achieving magnet status.

Red Button Game

Although management ordered Carmen Sanchez and Beretta Blowgun to stop bullying nurses, they soon returned to their old ways, with the CNAs bearing the brunt of their fury. Their shouting shook my confidence and made me look unprofessional in front of my patients and colleagues.

One bright and clear day at 11:00 a.m., I sat with a mentally ill patient named Mr. Edmonton, who was a suicide risk. I phoned Gloria, Mr. Edmonton's nurse, and asked her to please relieve me so I could take vital signs, since there weren't any floor CNAs that day.

Gloria said she'd break me after checking on two patients.

Almost immediately, Carmen slammed open the door to Mr. Edmonton's room and demanded to know why I wasn't taking vital signs. I explained.

"Forget Gloria!" she said. "You're taking them, *now!*"

I didn't know why Carmen was so angry. Usually, if we began collecting vitals roughly around eleven, she was satisfied.

Then Carmen said, "And why are you still sitting here, anyway? This sitter order's been discontinued."

It would have been nice if somebody had told *me*, considering *I* was the sitter. This was a typical example of charge nurses scolding CNAs because we weren't mind readers.

So I complied for seven out of the ten patients I'd been assigned, though not the other three because one had been discharged, one was off the unit undergoing a test or surgery, and one patient was in a medical conference with his family and team of doctors—this is a highly private event, and interrupting it was strictly verboten.

I made a mental note to return to Mr. Goddard in Room 19 after the conference broke up. Then I stayed busy helping nurses in rooms I wasn't assigned to cover, since I was now the only floor CNA. At 2:00 p.m., I felt an almost panicked hunger and headed for my lunch break. I'd been so busy and hungry, I forgot to circle back to Mr. Goddard.

During lunch, I remembered Mr. Goddard again, but when I finished eating at 2:30, I forgot again because I was desperate to take care of my assigned patients in Rooms 18 through 28 before I got off at 3:30. If I hadn't spent half the day as a sitter, I could have easily cared for these people, but now that I was on the floor, I was responsible for meeting their needs before I punched out.

As I headed for the time clock, Beretta Blowgun cornered me and said, "I just audited your vital signs, and there's many you failed to take!"

I acknowledged my one and only "honest mistake" with Mr. Goddard.

"Well, you really left that patient's nurse in the lurch and placed her patient in danger! This is inexcusable!"

"Sorry," I said. "I was swamped, and I forgot." I felt bad I'd failed to chart Mr. Goddard's information.

I went home feeling guilty but also furious Beretta had lied about my "many missed vital signs." I stared ahead from my couch, mentally repeating my mantra, *high pay, benefits, pension plan, high pay, benefits...*

First thing the next day, I approached Mr. Goddard's nurse, Gloria, and apologized to her.

Gloria frowned. "Allen, it wasn't a big deal. Mr. Goddard's stable, and I never said a word to Beretta."

"Thanks. That explains a lot," I said.

Shortly afterward, Alicia warned me Beretta was auditing all CNA charting, looking for signs of essential tasks not performed.

After my talk with Alicia, I passed ice water to all twenty-eight patients since I was the only floor CNA. Then I focused on caring for the ten patients I'd been specifically assigned. When I entered the room of my first patient, Mr. Ortega, a total care patient in Room 18, his nurse, Christina, shifted impatiently from foot to foot.

"Thank God you're here," she said. "Mr. Ortega needs a ton of care."

We worked on Mr. Ortega for the next hour. He was a short, overweight man who was developmentally delayed and contracted into a fetal position. His sheets were wet and smeared with feces. He fought us as we cleaned him and changed his linens and gown; then we struggled to feed and medicate him.

As we finished, I felt a rising panic. Beretta usually came in at 11:00 a.m. and worked a ten-hour shift, which gave us CNAs four hours to take care of our target patients before she arrived, but today she was there at 7:00 a.m. and was our sole charge nurse. I was desperate to service my assigned patients before Beretta checked up on me.

By noon, I'd cared for three of my target patients as well as many others who'd put on their call lights or had their nurses summon me. I'd also taken the vital signs for my assigned patients and was charting them when Beretta approached me at Nurse Station 3.

"How many of your target patients have you cared for?" she asked.

"Three," I said.

"What? Are you kidding me? Why are you so behind?"

I explained.

"That's ridiculous," she said. "You're lying. No patient requires an hour's worth of care. So, basically, you're telling me you've done nothing today."

Hatred rose in my heart. "No, what I'm saying is that I've been working hard non-stop since the moment I arrived," I said in a tone indicating I was ready for all-out war if she insisted on passing these lies up the chain of command. This did the trick—Beretta stomped off, but I was upset and had trouble focusing on my charting.

I took steps to clear my mind of Carmen's and Beretta's bullshit. During the warm weather, which is all seasons except for winter, I swam a mile every day after work in my community's outdoor Olympic pool. During the winter, I swam in an indoor pool. When I was a kid, comic books and swimming were the two ways I soothed myself when I was upset about the beatings my brother Danny and I suffered at the hands of our parents. And I remained comforted and invigorated by the soft, caressing water, the healing blue of sky and pool, and the wonderful buoyancy that made me feel as if I were flying.

I often wished I could retreat into a safe place when Carmen and Beretta upbraided me. I've owned box turtles from childhood to the present day. The turtle order, Testudines, is over 157 million years old, which means turtles have peacefully co-existed with other creatures since the days of the dinosaur. And turtles are survivors because virtually nothing can penetrate their hard shells. So sometimes, when Berretta Blowgun spewed lies and unfounded criticism at me, I tried to pretend I'd withdrawn into my shell, where her words couldn't reach me.

And sometimes I indulged in a highly satisfying fantasy. I'd pretend a tanned, handsome man in a white suit handed me a black remote control with a single red button. I'm not sure who he was, perhaps God or an angel or maybe just the new VP of HR.

"Think of a staff member who's doing more harm than good at Malmed," he said. "Then press the red button, and that person will no longer be working there."

My delighted mind instantly composed the list: Beretta, who screamed at everyone, destroying our morale and upsetting us so we lost focus on providing high-quality patient care; Carmen, for the same reasons; Donna, for the same reasons, plus her constant spying and ratting to Rose Oni added a whole new layer of toxicity to our already horrific work environment. Next came the nurses who mistreated patients: Pam Simpson, who was so emotionally cold that her patients assumed, perhaps correctly, that she hated them—and she was the one who refused to provide pain medication to a patient in agony until Mary Savage ordered her to do so after she'd ignored five requests to provide pain relief. And Virginia Black, who bathed a patient she disliked in cold water and rammed a suppository up the rectum of a sleeping and fragile old man. And Penny, who shouted at CNAs and patients alike. And, of course, Victor would've been on my list if he wasn't already gone.

The names rolled off my mental tongue like a sacred litany, and the red button game had a tremendously calming effect on me; it's kind of like counting bad nurses instead of sheep when one's drifting off to sleep.

Flip Side

Two weeks after Carmen chewed me out for not taking vital signs at eleven sharp, she spotted me eating a peach yogurt and apple snack by myself in the break room. She sat down across from me, looking nervous, her blue eyes watery, as if she might cry at the slightest provocation.

"Allen," she said. "Do you dislike working with me?"

"No," I lied, recovering from my surprise. "I feel like we get along pretty well, don't you?"

"Well, I just wondered," she said. "You know when I tell you to do something, I'm not angry or critical—I just want all of us to work as a team to provide high-quality patient care. That should be everyone's focus. I know I may sound angry or critical, but that's just how my voice comes out. I don't mean to sound harsh."

"I understand," I said. "Providing high-quality patient care is our number one goal and should be everyone's focus. And we should be working as a team." I parroted Carmen's remarks because I wanted her to know I agreed with her, and I also wanted to buy time to consider how honest I was willing to be in this discussion. Even though our words were awkward and stilted, this encounter felt real, and I wondered whether Carmen and I would reach a breakthrough moment in our relationship.

I thought about telling Carmen her tone of voice often made her sound as if she was furious, but I decided not to mention it, since she already seemed aware of it. I'd worked with Carmen for years, and I knew there was no way she could change her demeanor and tone of voice. Also, I believed Carmen was a good person at heart—I thought she made a poor charge nurse because she lacked management skills and the position made her almost unbearably anxious.

"Carmen, do you know I work hard and try my best every day?" I asked.

"Yes," she said. "I know that."

"Then we're fine," I said. "What makes me a little crazy are false accusations." I told her how I'd recently worked like a fiend from 7 to 12 as the only floor CNA, managing, despite my best efforts, to care for only three of my ten target patients during that time, and how Beretta Blowgun had accused me of not performing any work that day.

Carmen looked horrified. "That's terrible," she said. "She never should have said that to you."

"I agree," I said. "That's the kind of thing that makes me dislike a charge nurse—I know all of your instructions are meant to benefit our patients, so they're fine."

Carmen looked at me with grateful relief. "Thanks for talking with me. The reason I started this conversation is because of something Hannah said to me. I was about to leave for vacation, and I teasingly asked Hannah if she'd miss me. She said, 'Yes, I'll miss you, but Allen will be really happy you're gone.'"

"Carmen," I said. "Ignore what Hannah says, she likes to stir up trouble."

"Really?" Carmen said.

"Yes," I said. I gave her an example of how Hannah had said hurtful things to one of our housekeepers.

"This has been a good talk," she said. "I'm glad we had it."

"Me, too," I said truthfully. I knew Carmen probably would continue to bark out angry orders, but I felt a bit giddy she'd revealed her high opinion of me. It was almost as if I'd attained her protection. I was a good boy who no longer warranted punishment.

The next day, the hospital fired Carmen for violating a patient privacy law.

Red Letter Day

Feeling a bit more relaxed in the post-Carmen environment, I sat with a homeless patient named Luis Ramos. His night sitter, a young Asian man I didn't recognize named Alex Yee, stepped out into the hall to give me his report.

"So this guy's schizophrenic, and he goes psychotic on cocaine," he said. "Last night, the police found him in a car he'd broken into, and he was armed with a box cutter. He thought someone was trying to hunt him down and kill him, and he was in psychotic mode. He's on suicide watch. Also, I can't speak Spanish, but he apparently told one of the Spanish-speaking nurses he was going to kill her. However, looking on the bright side, he's on Haldol and in three-point restraints. They wanted to put him in four-point restraints, but he's got a bad wound on his right ankle. Have a nice day!"

Actually, I already was having a great day. This was virtually the only time in five years the emergency room had sent us an out-of-control mentally ill patient who already was on a sedative and restrained. As you well know by now, these measures were virtually never put into place until the patient had attacked and injured a CNA.

Using my limited Spanish, I said hello to Mr. Ramos, who gave me a friendly hello back. He was sunburned, his hands were filthy black, and I spotted numerous sores on his legs and feet, including his red and swollen right ankle with an infected open wound, which smelled, quite frankly, like a particularly pungent anus, a sweet and rotten odor we often encounter in the rooms of patients fighting nasty infections.

"Are you hungry?" I asked. "Would you like to order breakfast?" When he assented, I dialed the kitchen and placed the phone near his mouth and ear, and he ordered in Spanish. I talked briefly with the kitchen before I hung up.

"Your breakfast will be here in twenty minutes," I said. "Do you understand?"

"Yes," he said. "I speak a little English. Thank you."

Just then, his night shift nurse, Laura, signaled to me from the hallway. When I approached her, she whispered, "Watch out for this guy. He was a wild man last night. In the emergency room, they had him restrained with locking thick leather straps, and they used them on the gurney when he came up. Now we have him in soft restraints. Be careful—last night he had super-human strength, and it wouldn't surprise me if he can snap these soft restraints. Also, last night he told one of the nurses he was going to tear the glasses off her face, break them, and stab her to death with one of the earpieces. Sometimes he seems like a nice guy, but don't trust him under any circumstances."

I thanked her for the warning. I had a feeling this patient would attack me before my shift ended.

Back in Room 1, Luis signaled for me to release his restraints so he could go to the bathroom to pee. Instead, I supplied him with a urinal, which he used. Then he calmly waited for his breakfast. When it arrived, replete with metal silverware, I noted, I fed him his pancakes, sausage, and coffee. Luis thanked me several times while I fed him. *He's either a really good actor*, I thought. *Or the Haldol's working, or he's come down from his cocaine-induced psychosis.*

During the next couple of hours, Luis rested quietly, occasionally imploring me to remove his restraints.

At one point, just as I thought Luis might be over his aggressive period, he flung his phone and TV remote control against the wall with all his might. No, his restraints were still on for a good reason.

"If you stay calm," I said. "Your doctor will let us take them off."

He nodded his understanding.

When Alicia came to give me a morning break at 10:00 a.m., Luis once again indicated he wanted his restraints removed so he could go to the bathroom to pee.

Alicia spoke to him in Spanish, then consulted with his nurse in the hallway. She told me we had permission to take Luis to the bathroom.

"Okay," I said, hoping Alicia knew what she was doing. I admired her kind heart, but I also hoped she wasn't naïve. Alicia told me she'd never been hit hard enough by a patient to warrant reporting it, something that happened to me many times because I was often paired with our most hostile sitter patients.

We removed Luis' restraints, and he walked with difficulty to the bathroom. He didn't give us any trouble.

"Allen," Alicia said. "I have an idea. Why don't you go get wash-up supplies for him and then make him a fresh bed while I help bathe him at the sink?"

We executed this plan, then led a willing Luis back to bed, where he let us re-restrain him without any struggle.

When I took my break, I saw Virginia Black in the hallway.

"How's he doing?" she asked.

"Calm and cooperative today," I said. "Unlike the reports I got from the night nurses."

"Yes, I know," she said. "But if he stays calm, let him eat his lunch with his hands free, then restrain him again."

"Sure," I said, again certain I'd be struck or stabbed before the end of my shift. When Luis' lunch arrived, I removed his restraints. He ate and then allowed me to re-apply them. During the afternoon, he remained calm and cooperative. At one point, I led him to the bathroom to pee. When he finished, he insisted on sitting in one of the two easy chairs in his room. I sat next to him in the other chair. *Here it comes*, I thought. *Any minute he's going for my throat.*

But after ten minutes, Luis put himself back to bed and permitted me to reapply his restraints.

"Just stay calm, and we'll take them off soon," I said. "We appreciate your patience and good behavior."

"No *problemo*," he said. "Thanks for taking care of me."

Luis remained tranquil until 3:30 p.m. rolled around, and I was promptly relieved by CNA Jane, who'd come on duty at 3:00 p.m. and quickly completed her vital signs. This was a rare occurrence because day-shift sitters often weren't relieved by slow-moving evening-shift CNAs until 3:45 p.m. or later, and then we got chewed out for racking up overtime.

I gathered my lunch bag and punched out. In the elevator, I ran into Rachel, a loud CNA from Malmed's other med/surg unit. She knew her stuff, but she was also pretty crazy. I once watched her stand in a hallway and pretend like she was going to punch the arm or grab the crotch of every CNA, RN, and doctor who walked by. Everyone flinched and gave her a dirty look. I was surprised the doctors let her get away with this. One doctor who was deep in thought misinterpreted her hand movement.

"You need me?" he said. "Where's the emergency?"

"Hey! Allen!" she said in her high squeaky voice. "How was your day? Any crazy patients beat you up?"

"I thought that might happen, but it didn't," I said. "My patient was under sedation with restraints. How was *your* day?"

"Good. I sat with that crazy dementia lady who attacked you recently—Mary Woodcock?"

I remembered her—she was the wanderer who'd been fixated on assaulting the patient and family members in Room 5; she'd kicked and punched me when I steered her away from that room, and two nurses had grabbed her arms and dragged her screaming back to her room.

"Did you have to chase her through the halls for eight hours?" I asked.

"No. Today was perfect. Her nurse gave her some medicine right at 7:00 a.m., and she was calm and stayed in her room all day—no wandering or violence. She's being discharged into the custody of her sister. She's way better on this new medicine."

After Rachel and I split up in the parking garage to locate our cars, a warm, golden light suddenly washed through me. At first, I couldn't identify the feeling. Then I realized virtually everything had gone right that day. Two combative, mentally ill patients had been peaceful and content all day because the hospital had done virtually everything correctly.

Nobody had been attacked or injured. And although I knew this was undoubtedly a fluke, I fervently hoped the hospital had turned the corner and all our future days would resemble this one. I didn't even mind that my mentally ill patient had received metal silverware for breakfast and lunch—it was the only tangible reminder I'd indeed spent the day at Malmed Memorial.

Fall Guy

Anthony Warfield, a twenty-year-old ex-soldier who'd recently returned from Afghanistan, suffered from severe PTSD—his best friend had been blown up or shot to death during the war, and Anthony had been an up-close witness. After he returned home, spaced-out, he accidentally stepped into traffic and was struck by a car. He sustained a traumatic brain injury as well as a broken right ankle and a multitude of cuts and bruises.

This was about the sixth time I'd sat with Anthony in the previous two weeks. He was on complete bed rest, he required a CNA to feed him, and he either spoke nonsense, was unresponsive to conversation, or slept deeply for hours or a day at a time. If he needed to go to the bathroom, he was under doctors' orders to use a hand-held urinal or bedpan. Walking to the bathroom was strictly forbidden.

When I arrived at Anthony's room, night-shift CAN, Rebecca Morton, gave me a report.

"He's gotten a lot better in the last few days," she said. "He can feed himself, converse, and walk to the bathroom with an escort."

"How do I keep him safe when he walks?" I asked.

"No big deal," she said. "Just help him out of bed, put him on his walker, and escort him."

Anthony was asleep when I entered his room, so I sat quietly. A few minutes later, RN Helen Adebayo came in and wrote her name and phone number on Anthony's whiteboard. We said hello, but unlike our best nurses, Helen didn't provide me with any information about our patient, and I didn't ask for a report because Helen was one of the nurses who most mistreated the CNAs. I didn't want to give her the opportunity to say something insulting, accusatory, or bitingly sarcastic.

A couple of hours later, Anthony awoke and asked to be escorted to the bathroom. I helped him out of bed, placed him on his walker, and slowly walked him to the commode. Just as he was about to sit on the toilet, his right leg buckled, and he collapsed to the floor.

It's fairly easy to catch a falling patient because you can see and feel him start to lose balance, which you can quickly correct, but Anthony plummeted straight down like the proverbial ton of bricks. I'd tried to keep a firm grip on the back of his gown and one of his biceps, but he kept jerking away, not wanting to be touched and probably desiring to remain independent, an admirable goal in general.

So when he collapsed, I was surprised and horrified; no one had prepared me for this possibility. I asked if he was hurt.

As soon as he said he was okay, I opened his door and called for help, since, yet again, I hadn't been provided with a blue hospital cell phone, and Anthony didn't have a telephone in his room.

Helen Adebayo was the first to arrive. Instead of focusing on Anthony, who still sat in an awkward position on the floor, Helen shouted at me. "You moron!" she said. "How could you let him fall? Why didn't you put on the support boot for his right leg?"

I glanced around the room and spied the boot, which was partially hidden by fresh linen on a shelf below Anthony's TV.

"Because you and Rebecca failed to tell me about it. How am I supposed to put it on if I don't know about it?" My dislike for Helen turned to hatred.

"Can you please help me make sure the patient's okay?" I asked.

Helen finally focused on Anthony, who was unharmed. I put on his support boot and helped him onto the toilet. When he finished, I accompanied him safely back to bed and removed the boot.

Before she left, slamming the door and behind her, Helen said. "I'm reporting you for this."

"That's fine," I said. "Because I'm reporting you and Rebecca for withholding vital patient safety information."

A few minutes later, Rose Oni, my manager, banged on the door and then burst into the room, screaming at me.

"Allen, how could you let this patient fall? Why didn't you put on the support boot?"

"Because Helen and Rebecca didn't tell me about it. Rebecca told me to put Anthony on his walker and escort him, and Helen didn't give me any instructions at all."

"If you'd been a good CNA, you would've asked Helen for safety instructions," she said.

"Okay, my bad, but a good nurse would have told me about the boot." I didn't tell her I hadn't asked Helen for safety information because she mistreated CNAs at every opportunity. Besides, Rose already knew this and condoned it because Helen was part of Rose's clique, a group of bad nurses who constantly partied and went out to dinner with Rose and received "diplomatic immunity" from her for their misdeeds at work.

"I'm so angry right now, I can't even talk to you," she said, leaving the room.

And then it hit me: Rose was in hot water with Risk Management because we'd had three—now four—falls on our unit that month; I was her scapegoat.

To make a long story shorter, Rose returned to the room and shouted at me all over again. After that, Beretta Blowgun came in and yelled at me. She said I was incompetent and didn't know what I was doing when I sat with patients.

After work, I sought out Rose in her office in an attempt to make peace, but she was still furious.

"I'm so unhappy with your performance here," she said. "For one thing, you're constantly late, and I've already warned you about this once."

Total bullshit. I'd virtually never been late for work, and Rose had never spoken to me about being tardy. As for my performance, Rose gave me an excellent review each year, and I received $2 an hour raises, which I guessed were about the maximum annual increase allowed at our debt-burdened hospital. As soon as Rose started spewing lies at me, my "Spidey sense" tingled with danger. I could feel the frame-up snapping into place around me, but I didn't bother to fight it. As the Borg on *Star Trek* say, "Resistance is futile."

"And your letting that patient fall today is the last straw!"

"Rose," I said. "Two nurses withheld critical safety instructions from me."

She shook her head. "As the CNA sitter, it was your *duty* to draw out that information. That fall was one hundred percent *your* fault. You let another patient fall, and you'll be terminated. I've already reported you to Risk Management—I told them you have a history of letting patients fall, and they've instructed me to punish you for this one. Until further notice, you're banned from sitting with patients—you'll work the floor. No more easy days sitting."

No big deal, I thought. *I don't mind working the floor.* But I was angry about her lies to me and, especially, Risk Management. I swore I'd help bring her down if she were ever in a tenuous situation regarding her job or management position. And, of course, I added her to the red button game.

Hector, a CNA friend on another unit, once told me, "When Rose gets in trouble for something, she will turn one of her staff into a scapegoat faster than the speed of light. It's perhaps her greatest skill as a manager."

As for my history of patient falls, in my years of caring for hundreds of patients at Malmed, only one patient ever fell, but it *was* my fault. My unit once loaned me for a day to the hospital's other medical-surgical unit. There, the charge nurse assigned me to sit with a patient who'd nearly been beaten to death by lead pipe blows to his head.

He had a traumatic brain injury, and his doctors removed a portion of his skull so his brain could swell. Afraid the patient would waste away from nausea and lack of appetite, one of his doctors placed him on a medication called Marinol (dronabinol), a drug containing THC, the active ingredient in marijuana. The purpose of this prescription was to suppress nausea and stimulate appetite.

When I stepped into the patient's room, he stuffed a large handful of scrambled eggs into his mouth.

"The Marinol has made him food-crazed," his nurse, Carol Blankenship, said. "When he finishes eating, have someone remove his tray. And don't let him see any food after that, or he'll throw himself out of bed to get to it. If you have any trouble at all with him, please call me," she said, leaving the room.

I wondered how I was supposed to do that, considering neither the patient nor I had been provided with a hospital phone.

The patient's name was Ricky Alexander. Continuing to eat with his hands, he cleaned his plate, except for a tiny bit of scrambled eggs. When a member of the kitchen staff walked by the room, Ricky was either asleep or in a temporary stupor. Following Carol's instructions, I signaled for her to remove Ricky's meal tray. However, as she did so, the silverware clinked, and Ricky's eyes shot open as his tray disappeared out into the hall.

"Eggs!" Ricky shouted, rolling frantically in bed from one side rail to another, trying to throw himself out of bed to pursue the final scrap of his breakfast.

This continued for an hour. I pressed on Ricky's chest to keep him in bed while he tried to hit, kick, scratch, and bite me. If I took my hands away, he immediately rolled back and forth again, attempting to hurl himself over the side rails.

Several nurses looked into the room as they passed by, but they didn't seem to think my situation was urgent or any of their business.

I kept looking for Carol, but she never walked by. I didn't see any of the CNAs I knew on the unit, and, under stress, I couldn't remember the name of the clerk at the front desk, which was fairly close by. I didn't want to shout and make a scene; I had the situation under control, but it was concerning, and I was getting tired.

My thoughts kept returning to Carol's request to call her if I ran into trouble and the fact that I didn't have a hospital phone. It didn't occur to me to put on Ricky's call light to summon help. I felt like I was on my own, and I needed to calm Ricky down with food. So I did something stupid. I shot out of the room, grabbed a quick handful of snacks for Ricky in the nutrition room across the hall, and rushed back. Just as I re-entered his room, Ricky hurled himself over a bed rail and landed with a smack on his butt. Thank God he hadn't hit his head.

I felt sick with guilt and concern for Ricky. The number one duty of a sitter is to never abandon the patient, and I'd just broken that cardinal rule.

I reported what had happened, and Carol helped me get Ricky back in bed—turns out she'd been caring for an extremely ill elderly woman in the next room with the door shut the entire time. Carol reported the incident to Mary Savage, the unit's manager, as was required. The hospital performed a CT scan of Ricky's brain, which confirmed my observation that he hadn't struck his head.

When Mary Savage and my manager, Rose Oni, met with me, I provided an honest account of what occurred, and I got royally reamed out for abandoning my patient. I learned my lesson, and none of my patients had fallen since, until Anthony Warfield collapsed because he lacked the support boot of which I was unaware.

This single moment of misjudgment on my part with Ricky Alexander is what comprised my "history of letting patients fall" in Rose's report to Risk Management.

A final note about the Ricky Alexander case: As I was with him a few hours after his fall, his doctor came into his room and stood beside me, peering down at Ricky, who growled and slammed into the side rails, still attempting to throw himself over them.

The doctor regarded me sympathetically. "I heard what happened," she said. "And I can't help feeling it's my fault. That Marinol was a big mistake—we meant well, but it turned Ricky into a crazed zombie-like something you'd see on *The Walking Dead*. I'm really sorry about that—I'll discontinue it immediately."

Rose managed one final twist of the knife I didn't anticipate. By the time I returned to work the next day, Rose and Beretta had spread the rumor to the entire nursing staff that I'd committed an egregious error in Room 1 that resulted in Anthony's fall.

I figured this out when I knocked on Anthony's door so I could enter and take his vital signs. Standing nearby was Christina Phillips, a nurse I highly liked and respected and someone who'd always seemed to feel the same about me.

"Whoa, Allen," she said. "Are you sure you're even allowed to go into that room?"

"Sure," I said. "Why not?"

"I don't know, exactly," she said. "But we were all told you did something really bad in there yesterday that got you in trouble with Rose."

"Who do you trust more, Rose or me?" I said.

Christina thought for a second, then grinned. "I *knew* it was bullshit!"

Ultimatum

The night after Anthony Warfield fell, I was furious when I came home from work. I poured a pre-mixed margarita and drank it quickly, my mind racing with all the outrages I'd suffered: the screaming nurses, the frame-up by Rose, and getting in trouble with Risk Management.

"Bad day?" Elizabeth asked. She looked extra pretty—she'd gotten her neck-length strawberry blonde hair cut and frosted, and her blue eyes were as kind as ever. She finished chopping fresh vegetables for roasting.

"Yeah, really awful," I said. "But I know you don't want to hear about it."

"You're right—I'd prefer you to talk about it with Ginger, but if you have to get it off your chest right now, go ahead and tell me."

I poured a second margarita and told her everything. I tried to remain calm and matter of fact, but my rage kept getting the better of me. When I finished, I stared morosely into my empty glass, which Elizabeth gently removed from my grasp.

She put my tumbler into the dishwasher. "Here's why your work stories are so upsetting to me—you may not see it, but you're telling me the same story over and over again. You go to work expecting to be treated decently, and then you're surprised and outraged when you get treated like shit. You need to realize that getting treated like shit is the rule, not the exception. And you need to decide whether you can bear it or if you need to bail out."

She drew a breath, and said, "We need to have an adult conversation." Tears glazed her eyes. "I've been thinking about leaving you," she said. "Ever since you were hospitalized for a panic attack ten years ago, you've been a shadow of your former self, just a shut-down guy with no enthusiasm for life. You're a wonderful person, but you've got PTSD from child abuse, and now this job's killing you. You either swim every day after work to comfort yourself and I hardly see you, or you come home, toss back two margaritas, and brood over how much you hate your job. I want you to walk a couple of miles with me after work every day, and you need to overcome your PTSD and bad job. I don't want to leave you—I love you, and, frankly, I can't imagine you getting through life without me. I keep asking myself, who would take care of him? But something's got to change for the better soon, you understand?"

I nodded, speechless. I was shocked and heartbroken, but I understood. I needed to reach deep inside myself and resurrect the Allen with whom Elizabeth had fallen in love, or I could be doomed to a life of lonely misery.

Rebellion

The next day, Donna, our unit's vicious administrative assistant, sent me an email containing a preview of the hours being used to calculate my forthcoming paycheck. When I discerned her records showed me not working on a day I had and working on a day I'd had off, I sent her a quick, polite email pointing out the error.

Almost immediately, my phone rang, and Parker, our unit clerk, said, "Donna is up here at the front desk and would like to speak with you. Can you please come up?"

"Be right there," I said, puzzled why Donna hadn't simply emailed a reply.

When I arrived at Nurses' Station 1, Donna was already there, shaking a thin sheaf of papers and looking angry.

"What the hell was that email about?" she said. "I found it confusing."

"It's no big deal," I said. "It just looks like you reversed a couple of days on my paycheck preview. I was just sending you a friendly correction."

"Well, you listen up, Buster!" Donna shouted. "If your paycheck is messed up, it's *your* fault, not mine. *You're* the one who punches in, and *you're* the one who punches out, so *you're* the one who screwed up your paycheck."

Fury rose in my throat. "I don't have to stand here and listen to you yell at me," I said. "This conversation is over. When you cool down, we'll talk."

I walked away, but Donna followed me down the hall, continuing to berate me.

I whirled around to face her, and she jumped back, terrified. "This conversation is over!" I bellowed. "Get out of my face!"

"I'm telling Rose on you," she said with the whine of a six-year-old.

"I don't give a shit!" I said.

While Donna scurried off to report me to Rose, I took the elevator down to the next unit where my CNA friend, Hector, worked. I located him in the hallway, but I barely had time to explain what had just happened before Parker called and told me Rose wanted me in her office immediately.

"It's okay," Hector said. "Take some deep breaths. This is just typical hospital bullshit. You're a good CNA, and you take good care of your patients—that's all that matters. Be strong, and you'll get through this. Everyone knows Donna is a total bitch."

"But she's one of Rose's pets," I said.

Hector patted my shoulder. "Be strong," he repeated. "You'll be okay. Come see me afterward."

When I entered Rose's office, Donna was seated next to Rose, looking pleased with herself.

"Rose says you began shouting at her for no reason," Rose said. "Is this true?"

"No, quite the opposite, in fact," I said.

"Don't you *dare* lie to me," Rose said. "I can call witnesses."

"Call Parker," I said. "She was sitting right there when Donna started yelling at me for no good reason."

"That won't be necessary," Rose said. "Why did you yell at Donna?"

"Because she was already shouting at me, and I've had it. I'm sick of being yelled at. I work hard and I try my best. I take great care of my patients, and I'm fed up with your staff screaming at me that I'm lazy, or incompetent, or whatever. I'm not going to put up with it anymore. This is ridiculous. Don't you want to foster a professional environment?"

"I'll speak to my staff," Rose said stiffly, but we both knew that was bullshit. She was a screamer herself, and all her pets knew they had carte blanche to follow suit.

When I sought out Hector after I met with Rose and Donna, he said, "Well?"

"As we both knew would happen," I said. "Rose blamed me for everything, but I let her have it about the constant screaming."

"Good," he said. "You were strong. What're you going to do next?"

"Get the hell off my unit, maybe change hospitals altogether," I said.

"Try to change to another unit or a hospital we own," Hector said. "Don't walk away from the high pay and great benefits."

But I knew I was willing to walk away from anything to save my marriage.

Miracle

When I arrived home that evening, Elizabeth was basting barbecue sauce onto a filet of salmon resting on a soaked cedar plank.

"You're cooking on the grill tonight," she said. "Is that okay?"

"Sure," I said.

She cocked her head slightly, picking up on something in my voice. "Another bad day at work?" she asked.

"Yes," I said. "But we don't need to go into it. Basically, Donna yelled at me, and when I shouted back at her, she got me in trouble with Rose. Then I told Rose how sick I am of all the screaming on our unit."

"Do I need to worry about you losing your job?" she said.

"No," I said. "But I've decided to change units or hospitals. I'm calling in sick for tomorrow and starting my job hunt."

"I'm glad you've made a firm decision," she said. "I just hope we'll be okay moneywise."

True to my word, I stayed home the next day and contacted an award-winning firm that helped CNAs and RNs prepare resumes and cover letters. Soon, I'd sent them my former resume, filled out an extensive questionnaire, and participated in a ninety-minute phone interview. About a week later, killer resume in hand, I began a job hunt that included all hospitals within thirty miles of our house. At the same time, I talked with the head of Malmed's ICU, but she didn't anticipate any day-shift CNA positions opening for at least several years. I also struck out with transferring to our hospital's SDU and other hospitals that Malmed owned—Malmed had just hired a large group of CNAs a couple of months previously. Meanwhile, I received job alerts from all my easy-commute target hospitals as well as a steady stream of calls from recruiters.

I searched for a new position relentlessly for months, but a discouraging pattern emerged, one I'd seen before. First, if I applied for a full-time day-shift CNA position, I never received a reply. Second, if I applied for per diem work, I discovered I was only allowed to work eight days a month and without benefits. Supposedly, if I held such a position for several months, I'd be converted into a full-time employee.

To keep my current pay and benefits, I'd have to work seven days a week at two hospitals for several months before I could change employers, but I wasn't willing to do that. Also, Kaiser offered thirteen-week full-time contracts, but there was no guarantee of renewal.

These were the same barriers I'd encountered when I first realized Malmed was an appalling place to work, even though I now had five years of experience at a hospital that was supposed to be golden on one's resume because it indicated one was tough enough to work anywhere.

So I kept plugging away, waiting for a miracle. Presumably because of a massive number of complaints lodged against her, Malmed moved Beretta Blowgun, our remaining verbally abusive charge nurse, into an administrative position. She was instantly buried in so much paperwork that she stopped shouting at CNAs and

RNs. In addition, we acquired two new charge nurses, one of the highly liked and respected and neither of them screamers. Suddenly, the halls of our unit were quiet and peaceful.

Rose lost interest in taunting me, and, since standing up to her, I'd discovered a new toughness my co-workers seemed to sense and respect. When Rose wrote in my annual review that I was disrespectful to patients, their families, and my co-workers, I wrote a formal rebuttal saying the statement was not true, that I'd only raised my voice once, and that was when Donna shouted at me, unprovoked. Rose never disputed this correction of fact.

After my work environment remained calm in the months that followed, I pulled the plug on my job search, promising Elizabeth I'd work without complaint at Malmed for nine more years, when I could retire with a half-pension and full Social Security benefits. Especially if I could transfer into a more tranquil unit, such as our ICU.

After that, Elizabeth worried we'd lack the means to retire and be forced to work until we dropped dead. However, thanks to the hospital's pension plan, which included inexpensive but high-quality health insurance, our money manager assured us we could comfortably retire when I reached seventy.

And Elizabeth was coming around. She enjoyed a four-month medical leave following knee-replacement surgery; she said it was the most happy, free, and relaxed she'd felt in many years. I had a similar experience when I was out for six months on disability because of knee-replacement surgery and a broken wrist. We discussed bucket-list retirement destinations: trips to see our oldest son and his family in Japan, an Alaskan cruise, a tour of the San Juan Islands, a visit to Santa Fe, a stay on the Mediterranean...

So I vowed to Elizabeth I'd stick it out at Malmed. If I had bad days, I discussed them with Ginger Lightfoot, my therapist. Also, I swam only on my days off when Elizabeth was working, and I'd cut out my double-margarita ruminating. In addition, I went for a two-mile walk in an expansive sports park with Elizabeth and our beloved golden retriever, Ruby, every day after work. Elizabeth and I felt a renewed closeness as we strolled past the immaculate green playing fields beneath a soothing blue sky.

Punish the Innocent

One quiet Wednesday, I sat with a homeless man suffering from head trauma.

"He's been trying to leave the hospital all night," said Jane, a night-shift CNA, as I came on duty. "I finally got him to take a shower about 4:00 a.m., and that relaxed him, and he fell asleep, but I think he's going to try to leave as soon as he wakes up."

"Is he on a 5150 hold?" I asked. Patients who are not on 5150 or 5250 holds were free to leave the hospital.

"No," she said.

I glanced down at my assignment sheet, which didn't list my patient as having a 5150 status. When I examined his electronic chart, there wasn't any indication of a hold, either.

"He's polite," Jane said. "But he really wants to leave."

I checked out the patient, a muscular, middle-aged African American man sleeping in his street clothes with dark splashes of dried blood on the upper half of his bright red shirt.

"He's got head trauma," Jane said, "but he doesn't seem confused."

"Thanks, Jane," I said. "I'll take it from here."

Mr. Jamison slept until a member of the kitchen staff delivered his breakfast tray at 8:00 a.m., waking him. We exchanged good mornings. Then he sat on the edge of his bed and calmly ate his breakfast.

When he finished, he stood, wrapped a canary yellow "fall risk" blanket around his neck, and said, "I need to leave now. I've got to get back and protect my tent."

"Mr. Jamison," I said. "You've had a blow to your head. Your doctors want to make sure you've fully recovered. Can you at least talk to your doctor first?" Although non-5150 patients are free to discharge themselves, we like them to talk with their doctors first and sign a form indicating they're departing against medical advice (AMA).

"I'm fine," he said. "I really need to get back to my tent."

He strode down the hall, looking for the public elevator bank. As we passed Georgina, a CNA who'd floated to our unit that day, I said, "Please call Pam Simpson and tell her that her patient from Room 7 is eloping."

"Will do," she said.

Shortly afterward, we arrived at the main nurses' station facing the hallway leading to the public elevators.

"Parker," I said to the clerk. "This is Mr. Jamison from Room 7. He's Pam Simpson's patient, and he's decided to leave the hospital."

By now, Mr. Jamison was halfway to the elevators.

"Don't try to stop him," Parker said. "If you touch him, you could get fired. Is he a 5150?"

"No," I said.

"Well, I'm calling Security anyway. Does he have any IVs?"

"No," I said.

Parker called Security and handed me the phone so I could give a description, which I did.

"Is he a 5150?" the security guard asked.

"No," I said.

Then I walked to the elevator bank. Mr. Jamison was gone.

I circled the floor until I found Pam Simpson at Nurse Station 2, frantically flipping through pieces of paper in a file. Suddenly, she grabbed a sheet, scanned it, and said, "Shit! Mr. Jamison's a 5150! His doctor forgot to put the order in Soarian (our electronic charting system)."

She picked up the phone and called the sheriff's deputies, who'd already been in communication with Security.

"This to confirm that Mr. Jamison's on a 5150 hold. We just found out. Please stop him and bring him back."

While we waited for developments, I filled Pam in on what had happened on my end. She acknowledged I'd handled the situation properly.

Just then, one of the deputies called her back. I could hear his voice through the receiver.

"I'm sorry," he said. "We didn't know about the 5150 hold in time. Security saw but didn't stop the patient, and he walked up to the street and caught a shuttle bus. We know its destination, and we'll have deputies meet it at the other end."

"Shit!" Pam said, slamming down the phone. "He got away, and we're going to be in a giant amount of trouble."

"You and me?" I asked.

"No," she said. "The hospital."

This made sense to me. Earlier that week, a female dementia patient had been found dead in the stairwell of the power plant building of a hospital with a sprawling campus.[7] Five years earlier, another female patient had been discovered dead in the emergency stairwell of that same hospital—she'd been missing from her room for 17 days.[8] The word was the California Department of Public Health was cracking down on hospitals that "lost" patients.

During my five years at Malmed Memorial, my superiors repeatedly drilled the following message into my brain: *If anything unusual happens with a patient, immediately document it—if you don't document it, it didn't happen.* So as soon as I knew there was nothing else I could do to retrieve Mr. Jamison, I sat down next to Pam and electronically charted all relevant facts related to his escape. When I finished, I felt satisfied. Mr. Jamison had eloped as the result of a doctor's mistake. I'd handled the situation properly and carefully documented the events as I'd been trained. End of story.

But, of course, that wasn't the end of the story. For one thing, the deputies failed to locate Mr. Jamison after he escaped on the shuttle bus. Then I received a call at home that evening from Beretta Blowgun; she asked me if I knew Mr. Jamison was a 5150 patient when he eloped. I truthfully told her no.

The next day, Rose Oni, my manager, called me into her office. She was noticeably angry and upset. She asked me the same question, and I gave the same answer. I recounted the events of the previous day. I couldn't figure out what I'd done wrong or where this was leading.

"Here's the thing," Rose said. "We're being investigated by Risk Management, and we're trying to tell them a story about how Mr. Jamison eloped because a doctor forgot to order a 5150 status for him. Our story has a certain timeline, but the timestamp on your charting is messing up our timeline."

"I don't understand what I've done wrong," I said. "I did everything I could to prevent Mr. Jamison from eloping, given that nobody knew he was a 5150. After he was gone, I documented the incident, which is what I've been trained to do. Did I misstate something in my charting?"

"You had no right to document this event!" Rose shouted. "That was Pam's job. CNAs aren't allowed to chart anything about a patient who's left their care. The timestamp on your charting makes it look like we knew the patient was 5150 while he was eloping. We're having a hard time convincing Risk Management to believe our story."

Then it hit me—can you spell cover-up? Even though no nurse on our unit had made a mistake, Rose was under pressure from Risk Management, and she wanted to tell an ironclad story of our innocence. Somehow, my honest and accurate charting conflicted with the story she'd spun, one obviously containing at least one lie.

Reclamation

When Elizabeth and I got home from work one evening, we decided to have dinner out. We sat at the bar in our favorite local restaurant, a seating arrangement that always gives Elizabeth a thrill because she believes people who dine at the bar have the most fun. I never grow tired of her almost child-like excitement when we snag seats there. Over braised lamb shank, Elizabeth asked me how my day had been.

"Same old story," I said. "I did my job perfectly and got in trouble for it, but let's not talk about it."

"I'm really glad you've learned to take your job in stride," she said

I smiled. "Only took me five years," I said. "Even a worm learns!"

This latter was an expression I'd learned from my father. He claimed scientists once coerced an earthworm to wiggle down a straight path ending in a T-junction. If the worm turned right at the intersection, it received an electric shock; if it turned left, it was rewarded with food. According to my father, the worm went right ninety-nine times in a row and received a jolt. On its one-hundredth journey, the worm curved left and experienced a culinary reward, thus proving even a worm can learn. Whenever my father figured out something that was puzzling him, he'd cry out, "Ha! Even a worm learns!"

Elizabeth read my thoughts. "Speaking of your father," she said. "How's your therapy going?

"Ginger says I'm getting the upper hand on my PTSD," I said. "I used to have nightmares about my father grabbing me by the balls and totally controlling me, or he screamed at me and I wanted to scream back, but I could only manage a whisper. Now when he yells at me, I shout right back, and I often punch him in the face or stab or strangle him. It's all quite violent, but it shows I'm healing. As a matter of fact, I dreamed about him last night. We were facing each other, and I was in total control, trying to decide how to interact with him. A peaceful dream about my father is a good thing.

"Also," I said. "I've had several powerful dreams recently that weren't nightmares. In one, I find a red and gold box. When I open it, brilliant sunlight streams out, and I realize I've discovered the source of joy in the universe. In the other two, I'm dancing, filled with bliss."

"I'm glad you and Ginger think you're healing," she said. "And I hope it's true, but I don't think dreams are hard evidence of anything."

Given her abusive childhood, Elizabeth doesn't believe in anything that's not supported by concrete proof. Once, when she was a girl, she received a birthday party invitation from a girlfriend. Shortly before the celebration, her mother took her shopping for a party dress and a present for her buddy. When they returned home, Elizabeth sat on her front porch in her new outfit, holding her friend's gift (a stuffed animal snake), and waiting for her mother to drive her to her friend's house.

A few minutes later, her mother opened the front door. "You're not going to the party," she said.

That event occurred over fifty years ago, and my wife still doesn't know why her mother didn't allow her to join the birthday celebration. And even the new party dress and the wrapped present on her lap weren't reliable indicators that Elizabeth would attend the get-together.

Long familiar with my wife's skepticism, I smiled. "Don't worry about the details," I said. "Just know that Ginger and I believe I'm making good progress in shaking my PTSD."

"Whatever," she said, a teasing glimmer in her eye.

"Changing subjects," she said. "Remember how much we enjoyed seeing the whales and dolphins on our Santa Barbara vacation? I'm hoping you'd like to go whale watching in Monterey this Sunday."

"Sounds great," I said.

"Then it's a date," she said, smiling. "I'm so happy things are going back to normal for us!"

Renewal

On Sunday, Elizabeth and I boarded a white, sixty-five-foot whale watching vessel owned and operated by marine biologists. The day was sunny and warm. Although we entered a fog bank a few miles off the Monterey coast, we quickly passed through the mist, and we were comfortable in T-shirts, flannel shirts, and sweatpants, despite the rising breeze. Although we encountered a multitude of small rolling white-capped waves, the water overall was flat and gray with little chop.

After we'd been out to sea for an hour, we saw a humpback whale's fluked tail flash white on the horizon before disappearing back into the deep. Our captain adjusted the boat's course, and suddenly we were in a patch of ocean hosting sixteen breaching black humpback whales. The huge creatures burst from the water in graceful arcs, re-entering with minimal splashes. Nearby, another craft also cut its engines to bob and allow its passengers to observe the whales from a respectful distance.

However, humpbacks are curious and friendly, and soon six of the creatures circled the two vessels, people watching, and breaching in the same graceful arcs we'd been observing. Amazing, considering these leviathans are fifty feet long and weigh 80,000 pounds. Suddenly, one of the whales exploded out of the water right alongside our boat, a giant gleaming ebony wall punctuated by a penetrating eye that was wise and timeless, almost as one might imagine the eye of God or at least a god of the sea.

The whale plunged back into the brine. Elizabeth and I bowed our heads, thankful for this unexpected blessing. In the creature's wake, the ripples tipped us back and forth as the horizon swayed.

Laughing, we fell against each other in a tangle of arms and legs.

Afterword

COVID-19 and Malmed Memorial Hospital

At the end of February 2020, I resigned from Malmed Memorial and went to work for a high-quality medical center affiliated with the twelfth-ranked hospital in the U.S. Elizabeth and I were so overjoyed that we went out for a celebration dinner three nights in a row. Two weeks later, the community served by Malmed became a hot spot for COVID-19, and this remains true at the time of this writing. In addition, Malmed recently admitted a surge of inmates infected with the virus.

Of course, this led me to wonder how well Malmed was handling this influx of COVID-19 patients. The first thought that came to mind is the following story.

When I worked at Malmed, one of my patients came out of surgery and into the recovery room (PACU—post-anesthesia care unit) unable to breathe, apparently having an allergic reaction to one of the drugs administered during the procedure. Instantly, a swarm of doctors, nurses, and respiratory therapists surrounded him, rapidly trying out a wide variety of potential solutions to jump-start his breathing as the seconds ticked away and he moved down the path toward brain damage and death.

After all attempted solutions failed, a doctor called out for a "specific" scope that was unfamiliar to me. Team members franticly clawed through the items on the crash-cart, until one PACU staffer shouted that the only such scope resided in the emergency room. This person ran there and returned with the instrument. The team successfully intubated the patient, restored his breathing, and prevented brain damage and death.

After he rested quietly and the charged atmosphere calmed, I asked a respiratory therapist I knew, "What was that scope you guys needed so badly?"

"It enables us to very precisely intubate a patient." He shook his head in disgust. "It's idiotic that we don't have one in the PACU. We've pleaded with those administrative bastards for years, but they won't cough up the money for a second scope."

Back then, I wondered what would happen if two patients needed that scope simultaneously. Of course, now I'm speculating on the outcome when dozens of desperate COVID-19 patients might require life-saving devices at the same time. And even if the hospital committed to purchasing an adequate amount of high-quality gear associated with the treatment of COVID-19 patients, I worry that Malmed, along with superior medical facilities with the best of intentions and planning, may not be able to obtain this equipment, given the insufficient supply.

Related to this thought, I recently read a newspaper opinion piece written by a Malmed emergency room doctor regarding the hospital and COVID-19. In the editorial, he says Malmed's administration will have to "step up" to provide personal protective equipment, a safe environment to save lives, and the beds, ventilators, and equipment necessary to handle the coronavirus surge. Later in the article, he emphasizes that the COVID-19 care teams can't take proper care of their patients without "forcing the administration to help." Will the administration step up and provide the necessary level of assistance? I hope so.

Finally, I think about what it would be like for me to be back at Malmed right now, caring for coronavirus patients. Would I be reassigned to the emergency room, the ICU, or to a special COVID-19 care unit, or would I care for recovering patients on my regular medical-surgical floor? And would the patients be desperately ill and cooperative, or would they be recovering violent psych patients who are not sedated or restrained? If the latter, how would we perform effective infection control since these patients often wander the halls? And would I feel a strong sense of duty to care for these patients, and would I fear becoming ill myself? Just imagining myself back at Malmed fills me with dread.

Regarding my co-workers, I have faith that the CNAs and RNs I liked and respected would rise to the challenge of providing the best possible care for these patients. I'd like to believe that all the staff would step up as well.

I'm more of a spiritual person than a religious one. Still, I incline to ask that we pray for all parties who have and are still risking their health on the front lines: the administrators, the outstanding emergency room teams, the ICU teams, the red button nurses, their more compassionate and dedicated RN and CNA colleagues, and, of course, the unfortunate patients afflicted with COVID-19.

Allen Long
July 30, 2020

References

4:23—Stupidity and Lowest Bidders

1. "That famed John Glenn quote about a rocket's millions of lowest-bidder parts." https://www.marketwatch.com/story/that-famed-john-glenn-quote-about-a-rockets-2-million-lowest-bidder-parts-2016-12-11 *MARKETWATCH.com.* December 12, 2016.

Busted Up, Bruised, and Spent

2. "Busted up, bruised, and spent" is a lyric from Alex Bevan's song, "Rodeo Rider."

9, 14, 28

3. "How Baby Boomers Will Impact the Nursing Shortage." https://www.hhnmag.com/articles/7704-how-baby-boomers-will-impact-the-nursing-shortage *Hospitals & Health Networks Magazine.* October 6, 2016.

4. Barrett, Jessica. "The Impact of Baby Boomers on the Nursing Shortage." https://peopleelement.com/the-impact-of-baby-boomers-on-the-nursing-shortage/ *Peopleelement.com.* March 30, 2016.

Magnet Repelled

5. https://www.ucdmc.ucdavis.edu/nurse/magnet/faq.html UC Davis Medical Center.

6. Bachert, Alexandria. "Magnet Status: Superior Care or Marketing Gimmick? https://www.medpagetoday.com/nursing/nursing/68525 MedPage Today. October 13, 2017.

Punish the Innocent

7. Tchekmedyian, Alene. "Woman found dead in stairwell of San Francisco hospital property." http://www.latimes.com/local/lanow/la-me-ln-san-francisco-hospital-body-20180530-story.html *Los Angeles Times*. May 30, 2018.

8. Van Derbeken, Jaxon. "$3 million settlement over dead woman in S.F. General stairwell." https://www.sfgate.com/crime/article/3-million-settlement-in-Lynne-Spalding-case-at-5954050.php *SFgate.com*. December 14, 2014.

Acknowledgments

"Hell-Hole Room" first appeared in *Adelaide Literary Award Anthology 2019 Essays*. "Zodiac Dreams" first appeared in *Adelaide Voices Award Anthology 2018, Volume Two*. "Alex" and "Learning to Fly" first appeared in *Eunoia Review*. This book contains several brief excerpts from *Less than Human: a Memoir* by Allen Long (Black Rose Writing, 2016).

ABOUT THE AUTHOR

Allen Long was born in New York City and grew up in Arlington, Virginia. He is the author of *Less than Human: A Memoir* (Black Rose, 2016) and over twenty short stories and memoirs appearing in literary magazines. Allen holds a BA in journalism from Virginia Tech, an MA in fiction writing from Hollins University, and an MFA in fiction writing from the University of Arizona. An assistant editor at *Narrative Magazine* since 2007, Allen lives with his wife near San Francisco.

Made in the USA
Middletown, DE
19 April 2022

64400725R00102